Getting Lead-Bottomed
Administrators
Excited About
School Library Media Centers

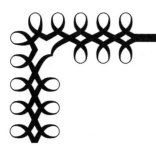

Getting Lead-Bottomed Administrators Excited About School Library Media Centers

TIMOTHY SNYDER

2000
Libraries Unlimited, Inc.
Englewood, Colorado

For all those who make a difference in the lives of children.

Libraries Unlimited, Inc.
P.O. Box 6633
Englewood, CO 80155-6633
1-800-237-6124
www.lu.com

Library of Congress Cataloging-in-Publication Data

Snyder, Timothy, 1949-
   Getting lead-bottomed administrators excited about school library media centers / Timothy Snyder.
      p. cm. -- (Building partnerships series)
   Includes index.
   ISBN 1-56308-794-4 (softbound)
   1. School libraries--Public relations--United States. 2. Instructional materials centers--Public relations--United States. I. Title. II. Series.

Z675.S3 S67 2000
027.8--dc21

99-089002

Contents

PART I: SETTING THE STAGE

CHAPTER 1—THE CHALLENGE 3

CHAPTER 2—ACCOUNTABILITY 9

CHAPTER 3—WHO ARE LIBRARIANS—REALLY? . . . 19

PART III: STRATEGIC IDEAS

List of Figures

Foreword

It doesn't hurt to have a little fun in life—and the title of this book points in that direction. Though whimsical, the term *lead-bottomed* is not one sought by my school-administrator colleagues. Neither is it championed by teachers, librarians, or any other educator. Unfortunately, however, it accurately describes too many of us.

Lead-bottomed administrators once served a worthwhile purpose. They did a good job furthering the long-held ideals and traditions of schooling in America. They were rocks, ships of stability. Everyone knew what the rules were and decisions were easy. Life was simpler.

But those times are past.

The face of public education is changing. America's penchant for criticism and finger-pointing, led by a hostile media and headline-hunting politicians, is creating an environment that is challenging at best and crippling at worst. Personal rights, choice, competition, test scores, and tax cuts are in. Personal responsibility and support for the common good are out.

Elitism is winning over egalitarianism. Children in poverty are losing their voice. Myopic parents with means react to the sound bite of the day and rush to create their own schools for their own children with their own agendas.

Public educators are struggling to survive in this arena. Gone are the days of producing a good product and accepting the respect of a grateful populace. Competition is in. So is business. Products must be new and improved and they must be marketed.

Discouraging, isn't it? Well, behind every challenge lurks opportunity!

Schools are adapting. The ranks of teachers, librarians, and administrators are filled with people who not only have the heart for kids but have the head for innovation. Examples of this new spirit of entrepreneurship in public schools are cropping up all over the country.

Public schools will not only survive, but they will thrive. The politicians will be right in one sense: competition will, in the long run, save public schools.

But it will only happen if school administrators get off their lead bottoms and seize the advantages of this new era. They might need some help.

That help could come from those people who have made so much difference in the quality of schools with so little fanfare: school librarians, library media specialists, library media teachers, professional librarians (or whatever else happens to be the term in vogue).

As test scores and accountability become the mantra, professional school librarians can step to the forefront of the effort to improve student achievement. They are more than the hub of learning, they are the generators, the sparks of accomplishment. They are the ones who, more than any other, have an opportunity to lead the teams that create the schools of the future.

Those teams should include building administrators—and professional librarians may be the ones to draw them in.

This book is written to the end that this might happen.

—Timothy D. Snyder
Reforming LBA

Acknowledgments

My world is filled with marvelous people who have contributed in so many ways to the small successes that have come my way. This book would not have been possible without their support, and I honor them.

Pat Wagner, author and consultant, paved the way through reference and inspiration. Betty Morris provided personal encouragement. Mary Vigil's proofing skills were indispensable.

Those librarians and administrators cited in the book helped more than they can know. Their enthusiasm for the causes of kids and literacy is inspiring.

The librarians who have served in my schools deserve credit for their patient instruction and understanding. Over the years, they have turned a rookie administrator into a flaming advocate for school libraries.

Last, my wonderful wife and best friend, Janis, has made life worth living.

Introduction

Libraries are wonderful places. Nothing matches the pleasure of wandering long aisles and leisurely browsing rows of books with intriguing titles. Images of history, romance, adventure, and exotic places capture imaginations and dispel time. The only difficulty is choosing what to read first.

Learning is an invisible by-product of reading for pleasure. Even the most recalcitrant souls, young and old, cannot resist insightful authors.

Who minds the gate to this treasure? Who steers young minds to knowledge? Do librarians really know everything? They certainly know that knowledge is power.

Librarians have inspired awe for centuries and this new century will be no different.

Our present Age of Information brings with it endless opportunities as it awaits exploration. Skilled navigators—today's professional librarians—lead the way.

These extraordinary public servants fulfill many roles. A typical day is filled with helping beginning readers or teaching research skills to older ones, utilizing technology, assisting individuals, coordinating interlibrary loans, preparing equipment, developing and analyzing budgets, attending meetings, establishing community outreach, and reading books from required reading lists. Librarians even find the time to help the shy kid over in the corner to find just the right book.

In these fast-paced, results-conscious times, libraries are more important than ever. Most educators have long been aware of the link between good libraries and good test scores. Research verifies that students attending schools with well-funded libraries achieve higher average reading test scores, regardless of parental poverty or education, than those who don't.

Students whose school libraries identify materials to be used with teacher-planned instructional units or collaborate with teachers in planning instructional units also achieve high reading scores.

Children who read for pleasure read better; students with access to libraries read more. Again, achievement goes up. Libraries staffed with professional librarians—qualified library media specialists—make a difference: children read twice as many books when professionals guide them.

But rough waters lie ahead. The government's cuts in school funding have forced schools to reassess their budgets, and school libraries are first to suffer. Such cuts are false economy. If a school's "profit" is measured by student achievement, it makes little sense to cut back on a valuable means of generating that profit.

Professional librarians know this. But do others—especially those fast-talking, super-ego school administrators who make decisions about the future of libraries?

The survival of school libraries depends on the commitment of its stakeholders, and the extent of that commitment rests with its professionals: They hold the keys to their destiny; they have the power to shape decisions. They can—and must—sell their programs to critical decision makers.

The ensuing chapters will help professional librarians do just that—sell the importance of library media center services to those who hold the purse strings.

This book is divided into three sections. Anecdotes and variety make it a fast-paced, enjoyable read.

The first section, *Setting the Stage*, explores the challenge and aspects of accountability that can be lost in the pressures of daily accomplishment. It details the personality characteristics found in those associated with school libraries and administration. The description of lead-bottomed administrators may strike a familiar chord with readers. The chapter citing examples of extraordinary library media specialists from around the country serves to transition the book from setting the stage to planning the action. Each example points out one or more themes common to success in the trenches.

Part II, *Planning for Success*, highlights various themes of success and instructs in each component of planning. Preliminary objectives, intelligence gathering, resource analysis and development, finalizing objectives, developing strategies and timelines, and plan implementation and evaluation are all covered in depth. A distinguishing feature of this section is the generous supply of examples and anecdotes. Readers will follow the lives of two professional librarians, Alan Reed and Terri Sanchez, as they exemplify the teaching points contained in each chapter to solve their particular problems.

The third and final section, *Strategic Ideas*, provides specific ideas to consider in building better relationships with administrators, teachers, parents, and students. Tips provide ideas for gaining credibility and for understanding how to achieve greater personal satisfaction.

Checklists and other instruments at the end of many of the chapters may also prove useful.

One issue difficult to deal with was what to call those wonderful people who have dedicated their lives to the causes of libraries, literacy, and learning. In speaking with representatives from different parts of the country, I heard several different terms: library media specialist, library media teacher, professional librarian, or just plain librarian. Readers will find these appellations used interchangeably throughout this book. Please know that each one refers to those who work so hard to lead and staff today's library media centers.

A final thought: The creation of this book has been tremendously invigorating. It has not only strengthened my appreciation for those who serve youth but has rededicated me toward their support.

The cause is just. Great libraries—and great librarians—are essential to the present and future success of our students.

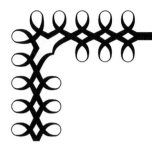

Part I

Setting the Stage

Read this section carefully. Enjoy the language and absorb the content. It is a necessary precursor for the instruction that follows.

*W*hile we can take justifiable pride in what our schools and colleges have historically accomplished. . . . The educational foundations of our society are presently being eroded by a rising tide of mediocrity that threatens our very future.

A Nation at Risk, D. Gardner et al. (1983)

CHAPTER

1

The Challenge

Working in public schools has always been tough, but now it's even tougher. Entire chapters would be needed to describe all the evidence of this—or the reasons—but suffice it to say that the rhetoric of headline-hunting politicians and blue-ribbon panels has done its job; public confidence is down and so are resources. Educators struggle with slashed budgets, fewer jobs, and downsized public schools.

Competition is in. Charters, vouchers, private academies, and profit-making schools are forming in record numbers. The public demands choice.

Elitism Versus Egalitarianism

Parents who once taught their children the values of personal responsibility now insist on personal guarantees—their children will have just the right teachers, the right curriculum, the right peers, and they will attend schools in just the right locations. Every child will be a star student and athlete, every child will be popular, and every child will go to just the right college and will certainly enjoy just the right career.

Sounds overdone? Although it may not be quite that bad, some say it underplays the situation.

Public education is struggling to maintain its position of respect and influence in a world increasingly governed by elitist ideals. Egalitarianism is waning. The fast-food mentality of a me-only generation now challenges public education in new ways.

Public schools will either respond or go out of business. Gone are the days of providing all children the opportunity for a solid education and calling it a job well done. Today's competitive climate calls for not only creating a superior product but selling it as well.

School Pressures

Public schools are better than they've ever been. In 1950, the high school graduation rate was 50 percent. Today it hovers around 80 percent. This means that today's public schools are educating youth who, in the 1950s, would have been relegated to factory jobs. These are the youth who typically don't enjoy middle-class standards of living. In current terms they are the immigrants, the poor, and the transient. They are the ones who require more time and more resources than middle-class children, who have historically succeeded in school.

Therein lies the rub. As public schools are asked to teach—and save—more of America's children, increasing numbers of affluent parents will look for ways to separate their children from the perceived negative influences of the poor; private schools serve that purpose.

Double incomes and fewer children per family are also creating an upper class that drives a push for schools of choice—roughly translating to schools that serve only the "right" students. Schools of choice that are in the public domain can even assuage the consciences of parents who want a private school environment without feeling as though they've abandoned the middle-class values of their own parents.

In fairness, affluent parents also feel the pinch as school resources, already inadequate, are siphoned off to teach greater numbers of children with special needs. This equates to fewer dollars for educating children without special needs.

Triage

Educational triage—deciding which students merit the highest priority for help—is increasing. As fiscal support for public schools continues to lag, and as more children come to school unprepared to learn, school authorities must make harder decisions as to who gets what.

Just as combat medics make life-and-death decisions about who will benefit most from the limited treatment available, educators are facing similar dilemmas. For instance, heated discussions erupt frequently over school budget shortfalls and the need to cut programs. Gifted students often bear the brunt of the budget scalpel. Talented student artists, actors, and musicians receive short shrift as well. Even in the best of times, few poor kids can afford a band instrument.

Emotionally disturbed children are more often than not warehoused in substandard programs because of the high costs associated with proper programming. Other special-needs students lack appropriate assistance, too.

Most visible in today's political climate, the push for improved test scores is pressuring schools to diagnose literacy deficiencies and aggressively prescribe remedies for them. Principals and teachers are targeting low-performing students, but then limited resources constrain action. This high-stakes assessment environment causes educators to make more businesslike decisions. The concept of diminishing returns comes into play. The result? While business clamors for efficiency and accountability, student casualties mount.

In addition, many students need more time in school to be successful. Too few schools have been able to raise the money to provide summer schooling for needy children. It's as if schools (hospitals) tell low-performing students (patients), "Sorry, the hospital's closed for the summer; see you next fall; hope you get well!"

Triage is fast evolving into an education metaphor, a climate in which all public school administrators, counselors, teachers, and professional librarians find themselves.

Effects on Library Media Centers

Great peril threatens school library media centers. Many decision makers consider libraries, in company with music, art, and other so-called ancillary areas, to be near the bottom of the school budget food chain. Money is available only for the most needed instructional and children-saving programs.

As if weathering the storms common to all educators weren't enough, technology is delivering a particularly hard punch to libraries. "Why," school administrators remark sagely, "the Internet will soon replace libraries. The world's information will be at the fingertips of every teacher and student right in the classroom, or even in the privacy of their own homes."

Many newer schools live this philosophy by downsizing library space.

The Challenge

This is the challenge. As a media-conscious, special-interest, results-oriented clientele clamors for attention, educators rooted in past traditions will be cast aside, and so will the institutions and programs they represent.

Successfully negotiating the rough waters of this tough political climate requires new skills and attitudes. Professional librarians savvy enough to seize—even create—opportunities to sell the importance of school library media centers perform inestimable services. They strengthen the link between information and learning. They improve the quality of life for present and future generations.

Summary

Today's educators face the challenges of media criticism, public criticism, clamor for competition, and an erosion of societal values. Elitism bears more sway than egalitarianism. Few recognize that schools are better today than they've ever been.

Triage, the practice of determining who is in most need of the limited resources available for education, is becoming a metaphor for public education. School library media centers are feeling this pressure as well as the twin effects of downsized budgets and increased technology requirements.

Professional librarians must acquire new skills and attitudes toward convincing a critical public—including school administrators—of the importance of library media centers.

The sea is dangerous and its storms terrible, but these obstacles have never been sufficient reason to remain ashore ... unlike the mediocre, intrepid spirits seek victory over those things that seem impossible ... it is with an iron will that they embark on the most daring of all endeavors ... to meet the shadowy future without fear and conquer the unknown.

Ferdinand Magellan (c. 1520)

CHAPTER

2

Accountability

We are the masters of our own ships. Each choice we make determines our course. We are responsible, in large part, for the successes or failures of our various enterprises. Neither school administrators nor professional librarians can evade this responsibility.

The Blame Game

All too often, educators adopt "this too shall pass" and "it's their fault" attitudes toward the bumps and jolts of life in public education. It is so easy to blame administrators, board members, legislators, students, parents, taxpayers, or just about anybody else. Seldom do we really examine our own roles and accept personal responsibility—and each time we shift the blame we lose an opportunity for personal growth.

Consider this anecdote:

There once was a library media specialist who was very secure within her own little world. She was blessed with a well-stocked library, an adequate budget, respectful students, friendly teachers, and an administrator who understood the value of libraries. Life was good.

Then one day a terrible thing happened. The district office called to say that so many students had been transferring to charter and private schools that a district school had to be eliminated. The bottom line? She was being sent to an older school across the tracks. Of course, the school across the tracks did not have adequate budgets, respectful students, or an administrator who cared one whit about libraries.

The library media specialist then had three choices; (1) she could bitterly complain about her lot in life and make everybody around her miserable as she worked in her new position, (2) she could bitterly complain about her lot in life while looking for a new job, or (3) she could use her new challenge as an opportunity for personal growth.

Of course, our heroine chose to follow the spirit of Helen Keller's admonition, "Life is either a daring adventure or nothing." She accepted the assignment, analyzed the situation, built relationships, and created a library media center that did great things for kids and teachers. She grew, professionally and personally.

Personal Characteristics

Although humans react differently to similar circumstances, we can shape personal reactions. The first step lies in understanding our own personalities. We've all taken the inventories that put us into different categories: left or right brained, introvert, extrovert, thinking, discerning, critical, accepting, concrete, abstract, Type A, Type B, explorer, pioneer, settler, and others. Entire study courses can be developed around these inventories and their application to the nuances of professional lives; they are useful in providing tips about understanding our behavior and how we observe and react to external events.

Although space in this book does not permit a comprehensive study, readers are, however, invited to review the following short stereotypical summaries and then determine which ones apply to them. (I know that it goes against the grain of any librarian worth his or her salt, but you may even want to mark them with a little check—in pencil of course!) Take special note of those that are similar, or other ways that a portion of one or more could be ascribed to the same person.

The following are listed in opposing pairs:

Left-brained. These are the teachers who prefer straight rows of desks and homework turned in on time. These are the professional librarians who store books and materials neatly in their places. Logic and order prevail. Accountants are most often left-brained; so are teachers. Teachers are usually products of left-brained schools: as students, they did their homework, didn't disrupt the class, and felt comfortable in that atmosphere. They then went on to become teachers and, thus, perpetuate the same system.

Right-brained. These are the drama, art, and band teachers. They are creative. Time means less to them. They enjoy thinking outside the boxes. More right-brained teachers are needed. They can connect with those students who can't be reached by traditional methods. They have difficulty, however, fitting in with their left-brained peers. Some professional librarians are right-brained; they can be detected by the amount of noise in their library media centers.

Introvert. Introverts would rather read a book than go to a party. They don't freely offer personal opinions. They may stay in the background but they are known for strong work ethics, too. Teachers aren't generally introverts but librarians often are, a trait manifested in their love of literature.

Extrovert. Gregarious by nature, extroverts love parties and avoid being alone. They can have strong work ethics but tend to lose sight of details.

Thinking. These are the people who think with their heads more than with their hearts. They are logical and they think problems through. Mathematicians, actuaries, and attorneys are thinkers. Although often difficult to work with, thinkers are nonetheless needed for their insight and down-to-earth thinking. They are task-oriented problem solvers. Slow, cautious, and deliberate, they often get bogged down in data. An interesting phenomenon occurs as thinkers age—particularly those with children and grandchildren: Their hearts soften and their tears flow.

Discerning. Discerning people think with their hearts more than with their heads. They contribute to humanity (not that thinkers don't!). Many teachers, social workers, and foster parents are discerning; they are particularly adept at reading the thoughts and motives of others. They are also sensitive to their own needs and tend toward more emotionality than others.

Critical. Critics form hasty opinions of others, stick to those opinions, and don't mind sharing them. They write letters to the editor. They make friends only with other critics. Critics are, however, useful to society because they interject reality when others have their heads in the clouds.

Accepting. People with this trait accept others for who they are and build strong relationships. School counselors are accepting. Sometimes they are accused of standing (agreeing) with so many ideas and people that they really stand for nothing. Accepting people are great supporters. They derive pleasure from helping others succeed and they make friends easily. They are oriented toward relationships and make loyal team members.

Concrete. Concrete people like straight lines and order, too. Engineers are concrete. One thought builds upon another. Concrete people understand the development and relationship of concepts and projects and generally see them through.

Abstract. Although definitely not ordered in their thinking, abstract people produce great—and unusual—thoughts. Creativity is their hallmark. They challenge concrete thinkers. They are fun to be around but can frustrate concrete thinkers.

Type A. Always on the go, these personalities take on multiple projects and somehow manage to get them done. They don't have much time for television and get cranky from time to time. They fill their lives with pressure. Workaholics by nature, they are the ones most likely to arrive at the gates of heaven wishing they had spent more time in the office.

Type B. These people are more laid back. They don't get too excited about deadlines and tend to enjoy life and live longer. They frequent theaters, symphonies, and amusement parks; they know how to relax and have fun. They can be valuable in work settings because they often figure out easier and better ways to solve problems.

The next three relate to each other:

Explorer. The inventors and dreamers of the world, explorers delve into new areas of thought and action. Wildlife biologists, geographic researchers, and astronauts fit into this category. Explorers don't hang around one place for long.

Pioneer. Pioneers may not generate the original thought, but they are willing to try it out. Pioneers have entrepreneurial spirit. They like building concepts and things. They stay on the job longer but get restless when the project is complete and the challenge of building gone.

Settler. Settlers are in for the long haul. They may not enjoy constructing the building, but manage it well once it is built.

Which ones fit best? Do you overlap from one to another? Are you a Type A introvert, an extroverted settler, or some other combination?

Most people cannot pigeonhole themselves into one category. It becomes a question of dominance as people tend more toward one side or another but, depending on the situations involved, may react with a latent characteristic.

Readers will also detect a bias in the language of this author's obviously not very scientific summaries of each attribute. Does this bias reflect certain personal orientations?

It could help, too, if readers contemplated their associates. What are their personality characteristics? Does this information help you to better understand them and, thus, lead and shape them?

Do not assume that people have the same behavior characteristics. Type A, concrete-thinking professional librarians cannot understand why their Type B, abstract-thinking administrators don't respond to written goals and timelines. Conversely, a thinking administrator often doesn't know how to handle discerning, emotional librarians and teachers. Serious consideration of these differences helps to improve relationships and, thus, better shape administrative decisions concerning professional librarians and their library media centers.

The above behavior categories are fairly well known and widely used. This next section presents four categories that may not be as well known but are in the public domain and are especially instructive in terms of school leadership.

Dr. Allan B. Ellis of Nova Southeastern University has worked extensively with leadership inventories; he uses an instrument, developed at the Northwest Regional Laboratory, that separates people into the categories of promoter, controller, supporter, analyzer, or combinations thereof. The following summarizes their on-the-job characteristics:

Promoter. Promoters will generally be eager to please others, especially those who respond to their outgoing ways. They attach themselves to people whom they admire and from whom they want recognition. They are imaginative, and respond well to incentives in the hope of being measured by their personal contributions. Promoters tend to get personally involved with others; because they often move rapidly from task to task, they will sometimes settle for less than the best out of a desire to get on to something else. Although they may not always like it, they work best in settings that provide structure. They need help with planning and follow-through because these activities are unnatural to them.

Controller. Controllers generally respond to a fast-moving challenge, and tend to get bored when the pace is too slow. They are task oriented, and may sometimes offend others with their eagerness to get the job done. Controllers want to know what's going on around them, be in the know, and help direct the course of the work group. Not having the situation under control raises their tension. They tend to set their objectives and work toward them without delay. Because controllers direct their energies toward task results, others tend to accept their authority and leadership.

Supporter. Supporters generally cooperate with and serve others. They tend to work through the structure to prevent interpersonal misunderstandings, and therefore accept supervision readily. They try to please others by doing what is expected, they like to be reassured that they are doing well, and they respond to personal attention from superiors. Because supporters do not like to hurt others or be disliked by them, they may sometimes withhold unpleasant information. To overcome their natural desire to continue working with the familiar, they often welcome direction from others. If they believe that their ideas can benefit others, they will put them forth in a nonthreatening manner.

Analyzer. Analyzers generally take an orderly, systematic approach to work. Being detailed and thorough people, they usually prefer rational and well-organized situations. They are likely to pause until they are sure the task is clear. Then they work at it with persistence, conscientiousness, and industriousness. Well-established rules and procedures create an environment in which their methodical efforts have the most effect. Analyzers may become tense, perhaps even immobilized, when surrounded by confusion or ambiguity. Because they are not likely to thrive on hard competition, they more naturally move toward advisory roles. Their steady and quiet manner will probably cause others to look to them for advice.

Again, a few moments of personal reflection relative to what category readers most closely align with may create insight not previously recognized. Likewise, contemplation of co-workers and their behavior characteristics will yield additional insight.

Learning Styles

How a person thinks and behaves directly applies to learning styles. Educators have long noted that some students are auditory learners while others are more visual learners. Still others are kinesthetic learners. Although we've all heard variations of the admonition, "Tell me and I may remember, show me and I will remember longer, help me do something and I will remember it longest," we must note that some people do indeed learn better by auditory means. School administrators can blanket their buildings with memos, but some of their staff won't respond until they hear it.

Caution

The caution in these behavior analyses is that we can't excuse our actions with a "that's just the way I am" response; that doesn't get the job done. We have to use the information to better understand ourselves and others so that we recognize weaknesses and use strengths in shaping decisions that affect us.

Personal accountability for success cannot be emphasized enough. The following words appear on the tomb of an Anglican bishop in the crypts of Westminster Abbey:

> When I was young and free and my imagination had no limits, I dreamed of changing the world. As I grew older and wiser, I discovered the world would not change, so I shortened my sights somewhat and decided to change only my country.
>
> But it, too, seemed immovable.
>
> As I grew into my twilight years, in one last desperate attempt, I settled for changing only my family, those closest to me, but alas, they would have none of it.
>
> And now as I lie on my deathbed, I suddenly realize: *If I had only changed my self first*, then by example I would have changed my family.
>
> From their inspiration and encouragement, I would then have been able to better my country and, who knows, I may have even changed the world.

We are the masters of our own ships. Every choice we make determines our course . . . and our destination. We are accountable.

Summary

Professional librarians and administrators alike are responsible, in large part, for the successes or failures of their various enterprises. Everyone has personal characteristics that affect the way they think or react to everyday situations. Professional librarians can shape decisions made about them or their programs by understanding and paying attention to these characteristics.

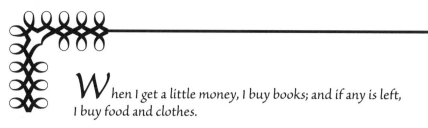

*W*hen I get a little money, I buy books; and if any is left, I buy food and clothes.

Erasmus

Who Are Librarians—Really?

There is some confusion about whether to call these awe-inspiring public servants "librarians," "library media specialists," or "library media teachers." The term *librarian* evokes images of steel-rimmed spectacles, perfect posture, and a sense of omniscience: librarians are the keepers of the dusty tomes of knowledge. On the other hand, *library media specialist* or *teacher* connotes technology and a sense of busyness, the director of a school's information hub. Both stereotypes are at once correct and wrong.

Keepers of Knowledge

Today's professional librarians are caught between two worlds. They must possess the knowledge that can be acquired only through the personal exploration of thousands of books. The ghosts of the world's best authors must reside in their minds, standing ready to yield their secrets when bidden. This is the old-world part. It has not changed.

Add to that the professional knowledge demanded of every professional librarian—cataloguing, collection acquisition and management, purchasing and operation of audiovisual equipment, researching skills, theme paper writing, oral reading, storytelling, curriculum, teaching techniques, budget development and management, and a host of others. It is no wonder that a full-service library media center must be staffed by a fully prepared professional librarian. Schools that try to get by solely with inadequately trained paraprofessionals perform a disservice to students and parents.

Change Agents

Today's professional librarians are also expected to be software engineers, automating their own domains while troubleshooting the technology ills of all who clamor for attention. They are asked to entice and teach children for whom the world of books and knowledge is foreign. They must be planners extraordinaire, plotting strategy to create resources and expend them to best effect. This is their new world. It swirls amidst chaos. It changes constantly.

Effecting change is no small feat—especially in school systems mired in tradition. The main problem is that teachers and administrators, for the most part, heavily resist personal change. They have chosen a career that offers the comfort of tradition with the security of a steady—although small—paycheck. They are not the least bit enthralled with the idea of changing their own styles or work habits to adapt to a changing society.

If change absolutely has to happen, however, teachers and administrators will first point to the need for someone else to bear the brunt. And that someone else is very likely the school librarian. After all, technology relates to information, and information is a library "thing." Kids who don't want to read is a library thing. If librarians are really *professional*, it is said, they should know how to motivate reluctant readers. Planning processes and projects should especially be the purview of librarians because they don't have to teach regular classes and thus have the time to do those kinds of things. And so it goes.

Perceptions

Librarians perceive themselves as overworked, underpaid, and unappreciated servants of society. They are the gatekeepers to knowledge. They struggle for recognition and support in a cause to bring the world of reading and knowledge to the mind of every child and parent.

The taxpaying public, on the other hand, often perceives librarians as introverts who enjoy the fantasy world of an endless cast of characters and settings provided by the world's authors. Librarians jealously guard buildings and books.

Because both descriptions are superficial, let's dig a little deeper. Who are professional librarians—really?

Answering that question may require a different type of examination. At a gathering of about 40 long-term and very successful professional librarians, the question was posed, "What started you on the path to becoming a librarian?" An interesting mix of responses emerged. Of course, a love of books and reading was foremost, but from there the paths diverged. About half spoke passionately about a librarian in their past who had taken a special interest in them and epitomized all that was good about public service. The other half ruefully recalled librarians in their past who had behaved as if they were library "wardens" and had displayed annoyance when asked for help in selecting or, horror of horrors, in checking out a book. This half got into the business in part to rectify past wrongs . . . to welcome all of humanity to a world of books and knowledge.

Characteristics

Although difficult to pigeonhole, professional librarians may share some common characteristics.

According to informal observation, professional librarians are most often left-brained and concrete-sequential. Their world demands order, and they have adapted themselves to that order. Their voracious reading, however, gives them such wide exposure to different ideas that they can display surprising creativity and entrepreneurship.

Although some are introverts by nature, they have learned that successful relationships provide an important key to mission accomplishment. In fact, readers who take the time to analyze the psyches and performances of professional librarians will note that, as a group, they have more successfully blended introversion and extroversion than any other profession. Those that started out as left-brained introverts have had to adopt right-brained extroverted ways to lead students to literacy and knowledge, coordinate curriculum and instruction with teachers, build support groups for libraries, and seek professional support from administrators. Those who started out as right-brained extroverts have had to adopt left-brained introverted ways to ensure the sense of order and task accomplishment that is necessary to manage extensive, complicated systems and collections along with budgets and personnel.

Given that blend, however, professional librarians have learned to be controllers. They have had to be task oriented. They have created visions of what they want their media centers to look like and they know what it takes to accomplish that.

Those using librarians' services should enjoy the pleasant demeanors and friendly smiles of these time-tested professionals, but should also understand that they have a purpose and will work hard to accomplish that purpose.

Depending on the situation, librarians exhibit the characteristics of promoters, supporters, analyzers, and controllers. They constantly "sell" books and knowledge, cheer on students in the quest for knowledge and growth, display insight into the minds and motivations of youth and teachers, and think like a Fortune 500 CEO in running the business of library media centers.

Above all, however, librarians are people. They share the bonds of humanity. They come from a variety of backgrounds. They are married, single, divorced, young, old, with children and without. They struggle with issues common to all.

(I have not, however, come across any who are swimming in wealth!)

Value to Society

Librarians' overarching value to society lies in their total commitment to the concept that every person has the right—and the responsibility—to pursue knowledge. Like Erasmus of old, today's professional librarians would rather read than eat, and they wish that every parent and child shared that commitment.

Summary

Today's professional librarians are bridging old and new expectations and stereotypes. As agents of change, they must assume more responsibility with fewer resources. They perceive themselves as overworked, underpaid, and unappreciated servants of society; that perception is most likely accurate.

Librarians have blended introversion and extroversion more successfully than has any other profession. Although primarily controllers, they must also, depending on the situation, exhibit the characteristics of promoters, supporters, and analyzers.

Their overarching value to society lies in their total commitment to the concept that every person has the right and responsibility to pursue knowledge.

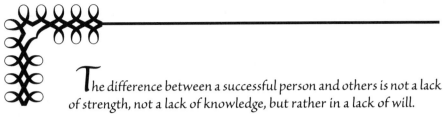

The difference between a successful person and others is not a lack of strength, not a lack of knowledge, but rather in a lack of will.

Vince Lombardi

Who Are Administrators— Really?

Lead-Bottomed Administrators

Lead-bottom. Descriptive, really: not overly critical, almost friendly. Hearkening back to the days of naval service, a ship's captain, after years of active command, would eventually be promoted to a staff job ashore. Working behind a desk was a far cry from the open sea. Politics, paperwork, and more paperwork.

Commanders used to the glory days of action and accomplishment adapted to shore duty as best they could. But the decisions were different. More people to consult, everyone looking over your shoulder.

Aboard ship, now *that* was the life. Free to act, a ship's captain had at his beck and call a hundred, two hundred, even a thousand sailors. Now, manning a desk, he finds the turf strange, the issues confusing. Even his image has altered: the morning mirror reflects a grayness and a blunting of his features. His step is slower. Decisions don't come as easily anymore. The decisiveness has gone. He has even heard subordinates referring to *old lead-bottom* as a mere reflection of his former self.

Does the term come with age, with responsibility, with a certain caution born of years of experience—and survival? Or is it a mental attitude reserved for issues that are unclear or beyond the scope of experience? Are there young lead-bottoms, too?

Regardless of reason, reality shows that many organizational administrators in schools and other entities today are definitely lead-bottomed when it comes to making decisions about library media centers. They intend no harm to professional librarians and their centers, but their very lack of action stifles progress and retards students' growth.

How many library media centers are governed by administrators in the lead-bottom category? What percentage—30, 40, 50?

Supercharged Administrators

To be fair, let's contrast the above—let the reader pick the percentage—with another type of administrator, the fast-talking, supercharged, get-them-up-the-hill leader who needs shaping to ensure good decisions concerning library resources. These folks can be effective library advocates, as long as they are supportive. But they can also be terribly damaging if, for any reason, they choose to go in other directions.

What's worse—the lead-bottomed administrator who needs a jump start to get anything done, or the supercharged ego working against library resources? It depends on the situation, a matter I will address in later sections of this book.

Characteristics of Administrators

In the meantime, further analysis of organizational administrators may yield important insights.

Like most people working in the public sector, school administrators think of themselves as overworked, underpaid, and unappreciated servants of society. Although they come from a variety of backgrounds, many are former coaches and military officers. In these times of school competition and choice especially, school boards are seeking organizational leaders with a history of leadership that may or may not be connected to schools.

There is also a trend among schools, districts, and boards to hire leaders who exemplify characteristics different from those of their previous leaders. For instance, a school or district that has already had a methodical and task-oriented leader may look for a new leader who brings a fresh outlook, someone who is creative and perhaps more abstract-random. Conversely, the district that has experienced upheaval created by too many fresh ideas may opt for someone who can settle down the organization and pay more attention to details.

Decisions related to the selection of school leaders can have important implications for those seeking more resources for library media centers. It behooves every library media specialist to secure a position on any committee formed to interview prospective administrators. Although it can be difficult from a single interview to gauge a candidate's level of library advocacy accurately, participation on the committee at least gives the opportunity to reinforce the importance and connection of literacy and library media centers.

Concerning the behavior characteristics stemming from Ellis's work, school leaders are most often controllers and promoters. Supporters and analyzers don't last long. Modern administration calls for creating a product and then selling it.

This means that administrators will want to be in the know and on the ground floor of any planning. They will be eager to get a job done and impatient with obstacles. They will be task oriented and thrive on challenge. They will also seek approval and be personally involved with others. They will like rewards.

Most controllers and promoters don't worry about the length of their workday. That's good, because school leaders seeking an eight-hour day don't make it. A sixty-hour week is about the minimum. Most need seventy or eighty hours to survive.

Work Environment

School administrators have egos. Living and working in a public fishbowl is not for the fainthearted. Those who seek positions of leadership often seek the limelight. They enjoy the challenge, the give-and-take of public leadership.

They even put up with the uncertainty of job tenure. A truism of administrative lore states that there are only two kinds of administrators—those who have been fired and those who are going to be fired. School administrators understand that personnel evaluation has little to do with contract renewal. The vicissitudes of politics can, and often do, dictate a termination and the resulting job hunt.

In short, administrators must embrace—or must have once embraced—the warrior spirit.

They also have a heart for children. Most entered the teaching profession because of a deeply held belief that the best way to make a difference in the world is to make a difference with a child.

Similarities

Professional librarians, professional administrators. Is there really such a difference between them? Both seek a better world for children, a world that revolves around knowledge. Both are seldom understood and most often unappreciated. Both like to control events within their own operations.

Working together, librarians and administrators can be an unbeatable team. They are strong; they are knowledgeable; they are determined. Indeed, they are achievers.

Summary

Lead-bottomed administrators, young or old, tend to let things happen. They intend no harm to library media teachers and their media centers, but their lack of action stifles progress and retards students' growth.

Supercharged administrators make things happen—even if those things are detrimental to school library media centers. They are only effective library media center advocates as long as they are supportive. They can cause great damage if they have a predilection against the purpose and potential for library media centers.

Both types of administrator need shaping by professional librarians.

The work environment for administrators can be difficult in that the vagaries of politics often result in instant termination. Professional librarians enjoy better job protection.

Most school administrators are controllers, as are many library media specialists—a challenging situation. By working together as a team, however, they can be unbeatable.

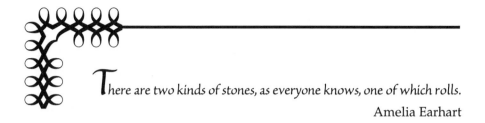

There are two kinds of stones, as everyone knows, one of which rolls.

Amelia Earhart

No Moss Here—
Success in the Trenches

eva efron

Meet eva efron—an energetic school librarian with an uppercase personality juxtaposed with the lowercase spelling of her name. With just over 30 years as a teacher and librarian, eva remains unyielding in her quest to serve children. During the course of a long-distance telephone interview, she performed a variety of other tasks in a manner that quickly led this author to understand that here was a woman used to accomplishment.

When recently confronted with developing a five-year plan for her school library (Brentwood High School, Suffolk County, Long Island), she sought an interview with her always-busy principal to make one thing very clear. Her message was, "If I'm to create a quality plan for our library, then I need to know your plan for this high school."

His response was revealing. Not only did he spend twice the time with her than had been anticipated, but he invited her to speak to his department heads. His message to them was, "I want you to be involved with the library."

In a large school, a statement of support such as this can go a long way toward strengthening the relationship of school librarians to teachers and students.

When asked about insights that she might share, eva offered a few tips. First on her list was the need for librarians to remember that, in her words, "Kids are kids." Regardless of their differences in backgrounds and attitudes, they share remarkably similar needs. School librarians must draw all kids in—not just those who are the best students.

Second, the best librarians are those who, in effect, manage by walking around (remember MBWA?). They know what's going on in the school, who is teaching what and when. They ask questions like, "Jane, what are you covering this week in your class?" Then they hustle to find materials that support that week's lessons. It's hard for a teacher to resist a librarian who says, "Here are some materials that may be of help to you this week. Enjoy."

Although eva recognizes that experience as a classroom teacher is invaluable to a school librarian, her school-administrator spouse has also given her additional insight. She even recommends that school librarians take a course or two in school administration to better understand the challenges of the other side of the fence.

Helen (Nitsa) Demos

Helen (Nitsa) Demos, a retired school library media specialist from Charleston, South Carolina, is a principal's dream come true. Never content with the status quo, this award-winning professional has garnered support in remarkable ways.

To create a flexible open library schedule for her media center, she implemented a campaign that few principals could withstand. First, she clipped professional articles and sent them to the principal on a weekly basis. But, before she sent them, she highlighted the most important sentences. Her reasoning? "No principal has time to read lengthy articles, but they will read a few sentences that promote what you're trying to accomplish."

Her next step was to arrange for a personal visit between her principal and the media specialist from a school that already had a successful open library schedule. The specialist particularly emphasized how well the flexible schedule helped her to better serve her faculty and students.

By this time, the principal was pretty convinced and ready to adopt the concept. However, because she was an experienced teacher herself, Nitsa went one step further. To foster the support of her own faculty, she invited a teacher from the school that was already using the flexible open library schedule to talk to her teachers about the advantages of flexible scheduling.

Then she worked hard to make sure that the concept paid off for all concerned.

With a heart for kids coupled with an understanding of her school's limited resources, Nitsa was always writing grant proposals. She put so much of her heart and soul into the research and discussions pertaining to them that her principal felt as much disappointment as she did whenever one wasn't funded. On one occasion, her principal took the unfunded concept to the district's language arts office and convinced them to put up the money. Another time, he persuaded the PTA to fund the remaining dollars needed to finish a project.

It is no wonder that Nitsa is still active as a media programs consultant—her enthusiasm is contagious. (See a later section in this book for a couple of her ideas on enticing teachers to preview new books. They are irresistible!)

Diane Oestreich

Diane Oestreich, Fullerton (California) Union High School librarian, is a soft-spoken person with loud ideas. Her story is one of fund-raising success in a state that 20 years ago led a tax-cutting wave that decimated public school funding.

Reviving a time-honored concept, she organized and led a "Friends of the High School Library" effort that, to put it mildly, has created extraordinary support for her district's six high school libraries.

Her plan was straightforward. First, their group of six librarians and twelve parents visited a nearby school that already had a successful friends-of-the-library organization. Next, they successfully petitioned the Fullerton Education Foundation to use them as a clearinghouse for any funds collected—thus ensuring tax deduction status for donors. Then they met often and worked hard to publicize their efforts.

Key to the group's effort was the creation of an initial goal. They needed $275,000 to automate district libraries fully; even more important was the support of two articulate parents, one a writer and attorney and the other his spouse, a fund-raiser for Cal State Fullerton. This couple not only taught the group the ins and outs of fund-raising but became its spokespeople and advocates as well.

The "friends" produced a brochure, revised it upon the advice of the schools' principals, and mailed it to each family in the district. They purchased a booth at the Fullerton Fourth of July celebration, and one of the librarians drew silhouettes as a fund-raiser.

They also promoted the premier showing of *Dream Rider* (starring James Earl Jones), a film scripted and directed by a Fullerton High School teacher.

Then lightning struck. California offered one-time grants to districts to use for nonrenewable projects; Fullerton's share was $600,000. Diane positioned herself on the budget study committee. Her erstwhile supporters attended that committee's meetings, plus the school board meeting, where they presented the library automation project. Their assaults were irresistible and the board agreed that the "friends" had indeed done their homework. The project was approved.

Some may call this luck. Others may call it timing. The fact is, however, that Diane and her group had created a vision and then a plan to make their vision happen. Only because they had put everything in place were they able to seize the opportunity as it came.

But that's not the end of the story. Not content with a single victory, Diane and her "friends" are in for the long haul. They have set other goals for library support and are working to accomplish them. For example, a fund-raiser at a local bookstore brought performing groups from each high school to dance and sing; coupons were distributed, which brought a percent of the profit on purchases.

As the campus coordinator of an alumni directory, Diane wrote the copy for the pages in the front and gave instructions for how people could make contributions to the school library media center. As a result, and in her own words, "When I came back from winter break this year, there was a $1000 check in an envelope in my mailbox with the memo 'library' right on the check. With the check was a form to fill out for matching funds from Shell Oil. I walked around for an hour, holding the check in my hand; I was *so* excited (still am!)."

Incidentally, Diane's narrative included a bit of advice: "Never, never, never go over the heads of either your campus or your district administrators! Get buy-in from everyone you possibly can; you can't do what you want to do without help and support from a variety of people."

Like Paul Harvey's *The Rest of the Story*, this next anecdote has two parts. Here's the first.

Al Sandrini

Al Sandrini has been superintendent of the Norris School District in Bakersfield, California, for over 15 years. During that time he has supported the development of a library program that serves students and teachers well. He has studied the links between good libraries and student achievement; evidence of that study can be seen in his remark, "A library is not a place to just store books. It is a place where kids can go to learn and where the librarian becomes a partner with the teacher."

Al reads a lot. When asked for specifics about his library philosophy, he quickly rattled off the titles (and ISBNs!) of several books about library development and then said, "It's my job to make the things in these volumes happen here."

Somewhat of an anomaly in the world of school administration, his support of libraries has attracted the attention of state policy makers. He has written articles promoting the value of libraries and now has a reputation as an advocate.

How did he get this way? What powerful force transformed Al from the ranks of a mere school administrator to a role of defender of the faith?

And now the rest of the story.

Beth Heisey

Enter Beth Heisey. Currently the librarian at Norris Middle School, Beth first met Al when he was a "somewhat younger" elementary principal and she taught in the same school. Their paths drifted apart but, years later, Al asked Beth for help. He wanted to put a real emphasis on improving his district's libraries but needed the right person to get the job done.

In Beth's words, "Since I had worked with Al before, I knew him to be a good listener and supporter of children and teachers."

Beth went to work. She sent Al things to read about libraries. Al not only read the items but sent many of them on to his board of education. This helped them to tune into library issues and they became supporters, too. They put into practice the things they read and, as a result, good things have happened in the Norris School District for libraries and kids—services have expanded and homework clubs started. LMCs are open longer hours and they have become the learning hub of each school.

Al's advice to new principals reflects his experience in educating children and also gives insight into his respect for Beth. "Find the most creative, hardest working person you can," he said, "and get them the resources they need to help teachers."

Mozelle Waters

Imagine a 98-pound version of an 87-year-old package of wisdom, wit, and experience in school library media centers and you will come close to understanding what a treat it was to interview Mozelle Waters. This extraordinary lady graduated from high school in Oklahoma at the age of 15 and finished college in the next three years. She gained her first teaching job by interviewing with board members out in their fields and convincing them of her talents. She taught in that small farming community for six years before marrying and beginning a 30-year career as a teacher and librarian at Jefferson Junior High in Albuquerque, New Mexico.

Although a teacher for the first 12 of her 36 years as an educator, Mozelle noted that she has always been a librarian at heart. "My life has just been bound up in books," she remarked. "I enjoy reading so much. One summer I read all the books in the 500s because I was weak in science. In fact, sometimes I think my database is on overload!" Although conversant in the vocabulary of today's technology, Mozelle laughingly points out that she was born "B.C."—before computers.

Mozelle emphasized the need for personal service in helping each child to love learning and books. "I knew every child in school and what reading level they were on. I knew every teacher and what they were teaching. I always had a cart load of civil war books ready before the history teacher asked for them. I did the same for the science teacher when he was ready to teach internal combustion."

She pointed out the importance of personal study in running a good library media center. "First you have to love books and be familiar with them; you have to know your subject. Then you have to know how to present it." One of the techniques she used to convince faculty of the importance of libraries was the analogy of an orange. "The orange peel is the building," she said, "the segments of the orange are the instructional departments, and the juice is the librarian—that's what holds the school together."

During her career, Mozelle visited and learned from school library media centers in Hawaii, Arkansas, and Australia.

Mozelle highlighted good people skills as necessary for good librarians. "You have to know the people with whom you are dealing, even study them," she observed. "If teachers have chips on their shoulders, don't try to knock them off—just pat them on their shoulders and go on."

Support from school administrators wasn't an issue for her as she talked about making friends with her superintendent and principals (she couldn't remember how many she had had over the years). She invited them to her library often and always couched any requests in terms of what students needed. She mentioned, too, that several of her fellow teachers later became principals and superintendents. Because they already knew what she was trying to accomplish with her library, they were naturally supportive.

One of her anecdotes?

"When I first started teaching, I was instructing sixth graders on what a collective noun was and gave the example of a 'team' of horses to indicate the group or collective nature of 'team.' Then I asked the children to think of examples from their own lives. One boy raised his hand and said 'rug.' When I responded with a bewildered look and asked how 'rug' could be a collective noun, he said, 'Well, my mother says that our rug collects all the dirt in town!' "

Mozelle had some advice for administrators: "Let others do the mundane work of the school and you get out of your office and circulate. You are the one who is supposed to know what is going on in every classroom and you can't do that if you aren't there."

Summary

Each of these outstanding people lives by the creed of famous world-class golfer Gary Player: "The harder I work, the luckier I get."

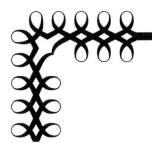

Part II

Planning for Success

Now the real work begins.

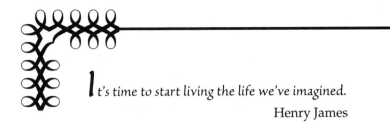

It's time to start living the life we've imagined.

Henry James

Themes Common to Success

Since the beginning of time, humankind has sought and found success in various forms. Military commanders, company presidents, and government leaders have arrived at the top—icons of influence, wealth, and success in a competitive world.

Millions of ordinary, run-of-the-mill taxpayers are also successful. Yet, for them, wealth and influence are relatively scarce. Obviously, their version of success is somewhat different.

Defining Success

Dictionaries define success in two ways. The first relates to achieving something desired; the second refers to gaining fame or prosperity. Most people opt for the first because it gets to the bedrock issue of life—the pursuit of happiness.

Although wealth, influence, and happiness are not necessarily exclusive of each other, most of us would choose happiness over the remaining two. Happiness can come in many forms, ranging from a child's delight in a gift to a parent's satisfaction at the sight of the child's delight. Happiness can reflect faith, most closely held thoughts and desires of the heart, and hopes and dreams for family and friends. It can reflect a passion for humanity, even for occupations.

Those who choose occupations aligned with their talents, hopes, and dreams are often happy. But happiness can be elusive. It is unique to each individual and it is an active choice in life. Consider this anecdote about life's choices:

The Law of the Harvest

Joseph Martin Apodaca was a teacher's dream. From the time he entered kindergarten in Lubbock, Texas, until he graduated at the top of his class at the Air Force Academy, "Joey" was a rare combination of work ethic and optimism. Not even the sourest teacher could resist Joey's charm, his warm smile, and his boundless enthusiasm for life.

More than his share of hurdles marked Joey's odyssey to success. The sixth child of immigrant parents, he spoke only Spanish when he started school. His mother and father, however, insisted that Joey and his siblings learn English as fast as they could. They even took them to the night classes the parents were taking so that they could all practice their new vocabulary together. The entire Apodaca family were rapid learners and soon spoke both English and Spanish in their home.

Life was good for the Apodacas. Although very poor, they had enough to eat and accepted the challenge of starting over in a new country. Mr. and Mrs. Apodaca believed in the American dream and taught their children the value of work. Mr. Apodaca was fond of gathering his children together and teaching them about the law of the harvest: "Children," he would say, "you get out of life what you put into it. You choose whether you will work hard or whether you will be lazy. Then you reap what you have sown. It's your choice."

When Joey was 10, Mr. Apodaca died in an accident at the farm where he worked. There was no insurance, and Joey's family was devastated. All the children were still in school and it would be a tough go for them to survive financially. After a time, Mrs. Apodaca gathered her children together and said, "Children, we reap what we sow. It's the law of the harvest. We can choose to be miserable or we can choose to be happy. Which will it be?"

That's when Joey's life really changed. He looked for odd jobs and was very proud to contribute to the jar on the top of the refrigerator that his mother kept for groceries. He swept floors and sidewalks for businesses; he mowed lawns; and he worked out a deal with a grocery store owner whereby he could help people with their groceries for tips. His employers knew that labor laws prohibited many of their arrangements with young Joey, but they knew his story and wanted very much to see him and his family succeed. They were thrilled to see a grade-school boy shoulder responsibility beyond his years and blinked their eyes at the petty rules of law that prohibited that progress.

Mrs. Apodaca was proud of all her children. They were a good family and worked hard together, with few complaints; anyone who did complain had to sing a song or two for the family's enjoyment. They were not a musically inclined family, and a few notes were enough to restore everyone's good humor.

The oldest child was a high school junior and wanted to drop out to take a full-time job. As was their custom, they held a family council and the choice was clear. The law of the harvest said that a high school diploma was important to future success.

Joey listened, worked and learned. His confidence grew as his teachers took advantage of his responsible ways by allowing him to tutor children just learning English. Joey liked to do this because he found that he learned even more by teaching others. He became known as a bright student.

Joey entered his high school years eager to succeed. Three Apodaca children had now graduated and were making their own way, although they all sent a little money home each month. Joey was still working and earning excellent grades.

Until his junior year.

One of his friends was giving Joey a ride to his after-school job when a speeding car ran a red light and plowed into the side where Joey was sitting. The ambulance rushed him to the trauma center and it didn't look good. Multiple fractures and unknown internal damage. Joey's eyes were closed, but he heard the surgeons discussing his case. He could tell they were giving up on him.

He had to take action.

He managed to raise his hand and call one of the surgeons over. He drew the surgeon's face close to his and said very softly, "I am Joseph Martin Apodaca and I come from a good family. We believe in the law of the harvest. Please work on me as hard as you can and I will live."

The boy's words and manner could not be denied. The surgeons went to work, and the rest is history. Yes, the recovery was lengthy and Joey's family and teachers had to spend a lot of time helping him out. But no one seemed to mind. He was a shoo-in for an academy appointment. The long process of physical therapy paid off and it was a great day when Joey passed his academy physical.

Four challenging years passed and it was time for the Academy graduation. The commandant of the Air Force Academy knew Joey's story, too, and asked him to speak at the ceremony.

"Distinguished guests," Joey began, "I'd like to tell you about the law of the harvest. My parents taught it to me when I was very young and I have never forgotten it. . . ."

Winning Characteristics

Successful people display many winning characteristics—thoughtfulness, attention to detail, goal orientation, work ethic, communication, people skills, and so on. The overarching themes common to success, however, can be synthesized into the following three:

Service

One of life's truisms states that "you love whom you serve." Librarians who make a conscious effort to serve children and teachers are the happiest.

Because service is the essence of libraries, professional librarians have to look a little harder for those extra-mile opportunities that can do so much to re-ignite the human spirit. One such act that happens in libraries every day has to do with book fairs.

Book fairs are great events. They draw students and parents to libraries and spark enthusiasm for books and literacy. There is almost a spirit of Christmas as children pore over brand-new covers and contemplate which to purchase. Understanding librarians are always on the alert for children who cannot buy a book. And, depending on the economics of the school's population, there can be many in that category.

The same librarians are ready for those children because they have already sought donations from Rotary and other service organizations to buy books for kids. Only the most cold-hearted businessperson can resist such a plea for help. Depending on the circumstances, some librarians have even provided small work opportunities for these children so that they not only get a book, but they gain the self-respect that comes from earning the book. Many positive personal relationships have resulted from this strategy.

One other point—there isn't a librarian alive who hasn't put up personal money to buy books for children and to supply their libraries with materials and equipment.

Intensity

Intensity born of a sense of mission and get-up-the-hill attitude matters. The best teachers are those who insist that their children learn. Librarians who insist that their libraries be successful leave a lasting legacy.

Intensity comes in many forms. Some librarians exhibit a strength of will that cannot be denied. Others have that strength but exercise it more subtly. The end result is the same, however. The job gets done, the goal accomplished.

Intensity reflects the lengths to which librarians go to *make* things happen as opposed to those who *wait* for things to happen. A couple of examples in my own career as a school administrator stand out in this regard.

Julie Herrera (at that time the librarian of Ortega Middle School in Alamosa, Colorado) was the one who really started me, the principal, on the road to support for librarians. She did all the things that most librarians do for their administrators—counsel, request, inform, plead—but one day she came up with the real key for me. She invited me to help her give a presentation at a regional conference for librarians. Now, most administrators can usually come up with a last-minute excuse for not attending a particular event, but it's a little tougher when he or she has made a commitment to help present. So I followed through, met some wonderful people (including Pat Wagner, who later got me started on this book), and got hooked on the world of libraries.

Another example is the triple-teaming that occurred when I was a superintendent later in my career. Three energetic school librarians—Priscilla Carinci, Andrith Davis, and Rosella Hood—made the case for automating their libraries. They had a plan and they presented it with such enthusiasm that there was no denying their request. I had to find some way to fund the project.

Entrepreneurship

Entrepreneurship, thinking out of the boxes, is a must in these changing times. Roger von Oech's *A Whack on the Side of the Head* gives worthwhile lessons on expanding personal creativity in problem solving. It is a must-read! Here is a tip that he quotes from Thomas Edison: "Make it a point to keep on the lookout for novel and interesting ideas that others have used successfully. Your idea has to be original only in its adaptation to the problem you are currently working on."

The following incident illustrates the intent of Edison's thought.

We had recently gutted the interior of an elementary school building with the idea of constructing a library in the center of the building and having the classrooms surround it. As members of the board of education and I surveyed the empty interior and concrete floors, one board member, Donn Vigil, noticed the outline of what used to be a "kiva," a three-tiered storytelling area that had been filled in with gravel and concrete many years before. He immediately made the intuitive leap and suggested that we excavate the old kiva and build our library around it.

The location was right and so was the idea. Everyone visiting that school today marvels at the mini-amphitheater (in use most of the day) in the children's library.

Enthusiasm

Enthusiasm binds service, intensity, and entrepreneurship. Enthusiasm challenges denial, overcomes opposition.

Tommy was an enthusiastic middle school student. One day, as he was spending a little extra time with his principal due to some misplaced enthusiasm, he watched as a young girl wept because she had accidentally dumped her orthodontic retainer in the trash barrel along with her leftover cafeteria food. Tommy leaped to the rescue and shot a deal to the principal: "If I go through the garbage barrel and find the retainer, will you let me go out and play?" The principal agreed.

Tommy was almost upended in the garbage for 10 minutes before he emerged triumphantly. "I found it!" he exclaimed. The little girl's face turned to a smile as Tommy handed her the retainer.

Tommy was almost out the door when she wailed, "But this isn't my retainer!"

Though they never found the girl's retainer, or the owner of the found one, Tommy's enthusiasm won him a trip outdoors.

Summary

Personal attitudes create happiness, which equates to success. The law of the harvest promises reward for hard work. Themes common to success are service, intensity, and entrepreneurship. Enthusiasm helps it all to happen.

I realized that if what we call human nature can be changed, then absolutely anything is possible. From that moment, my life changed.

Shirley MacLaine

Planning for Success

Most mortals travel through life with very little sense of direction. Tossed about by the vagaries of life, they take little thought toward where they've been, where they are right now, and where they'd like to be tomorrow. After all, schedules have to be kept, appointments made, and things just have to be done.

Contemplation

Thinking, the quiet contemplation of issues so important to inner peace, satisfaction, and personal progress, is becoming a lost art. Moments most conducive to thought succumb to telephones, television, and those wonderful, time-eating devices of technology, personal computers, accompanied of course by

Internet connectivity and a gigazillion games. (It is no wonder that the as-yet-unnamed generation-to-come aspires to new lows of hyperkinetic media attachment.)

But it's hard. Thoughtful people are rare because blocking out time demands real commitment. Plus, in these fast-paced, frenetic times, a sort of dubious honor attaches itself to busyness. However, although work enobles the mind and action accomplishes goals, finding (creating?) the time to *think* bestows a gift of great value. The following analogy applies.

In a competition (originating in Sweden) called "orienteering," runners are given topographic maps with checkpoints marked on an approximately 10-mile outdoor course. The competitor who finds the checkpoints (and can produce the required evidence—description of the marker, special punchmark, etc.) in the least amount of time wins the race. Often, it is not the fleetest of foot who wins but the best planner and most skilled map reader. Why? Because the quickest way to travel from point A to point B is sometimes not the shortest way. Hills, rivers, and cliffs consume time. Competitors who take the time to carefully review their maps and plot an accurate course most often win.

Less Is More

Mahatma Gandhi said, "There is more to life than increasing its speed." In other words, less really can be more, a profound concept with important implications for success in any endeavor.

Consider this: people who can fully concentrate on a single problem for three minutes can accomplish anything. They have the power to shape the world, or at least their own environments. This means that professional librarians can shape their working conditions. They can influence people and events. They can create their own destinies. All it takes is good, focused thought, which then becomes the genesis of that most important vehicle for success—the plan.

Hierarchy of Planning

Planning is a hierarchy. Lower-order plans come from minimal thought and have minimal consequences. Acquisition plans, automation plans, and plans for weeding and organizing fall into this category. So do daily lesson plans. Although these are important and necessary functions, they are more concerned with management responsibilities, the day-to-day operations of libraries.

The real fun—and the lasting legacy of any professional librarian—lies in the ability to create higher-order plans. These plans involve leadership. They require thought, and lots of it. They require savvy—that unique combination of judgment and timeliness so critical to successful accomplishment. Plans that display a dash of zest and flair for life are even better.

There is no substitute for personal, thorough planning. Good librarians can become great through its exercise. Committees have their place but they are no substitute. Supportive teachers and principals can help, but they are no substitute. Library advocacy groups are wonderful, but they are no substitute. There is power in personal, higher-order planning.

"Those who fail to plan, plan to fail" is a time-worn phrase, but is true nonetheless. The vagaries of life continue to toss those who refuse to wrest away moments of contemplation and consideration, so vital to planning.

Perhaps Will Rogers voiced a more appropriate thought: "Even if you're on the right track, you'll get run over if you just sit there." Good librarians are on the right track. Great librarians lead the way.

Planning is essential to success.

The Components
of Successful Planning

General George S. Patton succinctly stated the case for planning with his oft-repeated injunction, "A pint of sweat will save a gallon of blood."

Although military genre is not typically the province of librarians, the following narrative may nonetheless prove useful for two reasons—it details the components of successful planning and gives insight into the minds of school administrators having military backgrounds. Schools across the country are increasingly reaching out to retired military officers for leadership, and librarians who know something about them could have an edge.

The Assault

The stench of sweat mingled with the odor of half-eaten C-rations filled the sweltering bunker. The floor was dirt, the furnishings sparse. A single light bulb hung from the timbered ceiling, providing a pittance of illumination. It was night and unusually quiet; only the high-pitched whine of an occasional mosquito and the muffled voices of tired radio operators punctuated the monotony.

Within spitting distance of Vietnam's DMZ, the sandbagged edifice was the command center of the Third Battalion, Third Marines.

Lieutenant Colonel Mike Steele pored over the map spread before him, his lined face betraying worry and lack of sleep. His immediate superior, the regimental commander, had just called with tomorrow's mission—attack and seize Hill 411 by no later than 1500 Hours.

Steele considered the enormity of what lay ahead. A long march, rough terrain, and dug-in enemy were a challenge; but capturing the hill with minimal casualties presented an even more formidable task. After only six months as battalion commander, he was already tired of writing condolence letters to the parents of Marines—his Marines—killed in action.

Dear Mr. and Mrs. Jones: I regret to inform you that your son, Private First Class Robert Jones, was killed on May 22, 1968, while participating in action against the enemy in Quang Tri Province, the Republic of South Vietnam. Bobby, as he was known by his many friends, was . . .

Refusing to bow to emotion, Steele returned to the task at hand and rehearsed the components of battle planning, drilled into his mind by countless instructors. They all preached the same message. *Know your objective, know your enemy, know your resources, determine the strategies and timeline of your plan, execute your plan, and evaluate it afterwards.*

He knew his objective. Hill 411. He knew the parameters. Be there by 1500 Hours tomorrow. Maximize enemy casualties. Minimize friendly casualties.

What did he know about the enemy, about the situation? As he studied the map, he recognized the terrain. He'd led patrols over it before. Rough ground, a few open areas, two streams, a 10-kilometer march, then the hill. Not much of one really, but lots of cover and concealment for a dug-in enemy. Another caution from voices past: *the advantage always rests with the defense.*

How many enemy? The soothsayers from intelligence said a full company of the North Vietnamese Army (NVA), over 100 well-fed and well-equipped troops. No Viet Cong. They don't usually come this far north.

He allowed himself a small smile. His civilian friends back home would say that "military intelligence" was a contradiction in terms. It was too bad they weren't here with him now. Easy criticism tends to melt in the heat of battle.

Steele pondered the mission of the NVA company. Why were they there and how bad did they want to stay? He had been on that hill two weeks earlier and it was unoccupied then.

He thought about the exact location of the NVA. If he were their commander, where would he place them? At the top, the easiest to defend, with listening posts downslope. Crew-served weapons on the flanks. Underground bunkers and fighting holes connected by tunnels. *The advantage rests with the defense.*

He jotted down his own resources. Four companies—India, Kilo, Lima and Mike, with close to 150 men in each. Two fresh company commanders, mostly seasoned troops. Morale reasonable. A weapons platoon with mortars and extra machine guns.

The weather would help. It would be hot, but the clouds high. Air support could get in. How he exulted when swooping jet fighters, screaming low over the treetops, dealt their own versions of death and destruction. Every dead NVA meant one less who could kill a Marine.

Artillery and naval gunfire should be available, too. Maybe he could get help from the *Missouri*, cruising just offshore with its 16-inch guns. Timing and fire priorities would be crucial.

Steele saw his strategies emerge.

An early departure would allow for unexpected delays. Need to reach assembly point by mid-morning. Rations and ammunition for two days would suffice—excess weight impacts movement. Communications are important. Extra batteries vital.

Begin prep fire at 1100 Hours. Hit them for 30 minutes with artillery from the *Missouri* and/or the fire support base. Try to get a pass or two from the fighters. Napalm may do some damage.

Send India Company up the middle. It's their turn and they're ready. Have India engage and then strike at both southern flanks with Kilo and Lima. Hold Mike in reserve. The command center will go with India. *Lead from the front. Never send your men where you won't go yourself.*

Steele sketched out the plan and called for his operations officer. There was work to be done—unit leaders to inform, gear to check, and times to coordinate with support groups. In another hour, the battle plan would be refined and documented.

The Takeover

Sounds a little cheesy, doesn't it? That must be why I'm in the school business and not in the action novel business! Of course, the story could have started like this:

Nancy Steele hung up the phone and glanced quickly at the clock on her beautifully appointed cherry desk. Her boss was a stickler for punctuality and she had only an hour left to finish the plan. She was excited about it. The chance to gain majority control over Acme Manufacturing was too good to pass up. Her plan would be the blueprint for the operation.

The Big Game

Or how about this?

Coach Jim Steele looked his star athlete in the eye and spat out, "You know the plan, kid! Get in there and get it done!"

Summary

Quiet, contemplative time is hard to create in these frenetic times, but it is crucial to plan development. Effective planning can save problems while accomplishing many lower- and higher-order missions.

These are the seven components of planning (see Figure 7.1, page 56): determining the preliminary objective, gathering intelligence, identifying and developing resources, finalizing objectives, developing strategies and timelines, implementing the plan, and evaluating the plan. They are essential to success in any endeavor and no plan can be complete without any one of them. Ensuing chapters will explain them in detail.

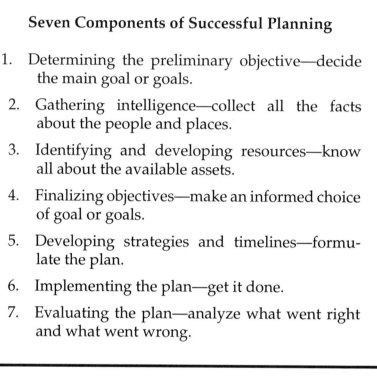

Seven Components of Successful Planning

1. Determining the preliminary objective—decide the main goal or goals.

2. Gathering intelligence—collect all the facts about the people and places.

3. Identifying and developing resources—know all about the available assets.

4. Finalizing objectives—make an informed choice of goal or goals.

5. Developing strategies and timelines—formulate the plan.

6. Implementing the plan—get it done.

7. Evaluating the plan—analyze what went right and what went wrong.

Figure 7.1 Seven components of successful planning.

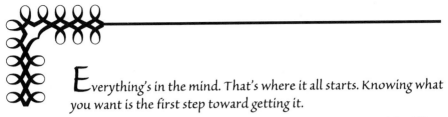

Everything's in the mind. That's where it all starts. Knowing what you want is the first step toward getting it.

Mae West

The Preliminary Objective

Preliminary objectives are fluid. Subject to instant change, they can reflect idle whim or focused thought. However meaningful—or meaningless—their origin, they are critical to the outcome of any plan because they provide a starting point.

The following shows one reason starting points make all-important differences in outcomes.

Diverging Paths

The mid-nineteenth century witnessed a great westward migration across the North American continent. Entire companies of wagon trains traveled the long, hard miles of the Oregon

Trail searching for new lands and new futures. The Mormon Trail paralleled the Oregon Trail for the first 500 miles and then, in southwestern Wyoming, branched off toward Utah. Pioneer journals record the observations of the men and women walking this route. They note that, at first, the separation was barely noticeable. After one mile, members of two diverging wagon trains could still wave and be recognized. After a few miles, they were no longer visible to each other.

As penned by Robert Frost, two paths can, indeed, lead in very different directions.

For example, Mrs. Jones, a professional librarian in an urban school, noticed one day a youth surreptitiously writing in a book, placing it back on the shelf, and then quickly leaving the premises. A naturally curious individual, she walked over to the book and looked to see what the boy had written. She was extremely displeased to find vulgarities laced with gang symbols. Aware that vandalism was a growing problem in her library, she found a quiet place and concentrated for three full minutes on how she might resolve the problem.

A variety of thoughts ran through her mind and synthesized into two distinct paths. One, she could take the fortress approach or, two, she could go on the offensive.

The fortress approach would call for stepped-up communications to students concerning the consequences of defacing library property. Surveillance cameras would monitor the building. Volunteer "deputies" would patrol the premises. Martial law would rule.

Going on the offensive would require more planning and perhaps even risk. Reasons for the gang writing would have to be explored. Statistics analyzed. Interviews conducted. In short, would there be any possibility of getting to the heart of—and resolving—the basic issues rather than just reacting to the symptoms?

Ownership

Of course, this type of analysis presupposes ownership of the problem. It opens the door to the possibility that the philosophies and procedures of the library and/or the librarian may be contributing to the problem; indeed, close examination can sometimes yield surprising results. As a hard-charging high school principal, I once had my comeuppance in a scenario that applies to this concept.

A teacher struggling with classroom control asked me to teach her class one day so that she could observe and pick up some new techniques. A natural ham, I not only agreed but asked that she make arrangements for videotaping so that I could evaluate my own teaching too.

The day came and I taught what I assumed to be a fairly good class. Students seemed to be engaged and, by the end of the class, reasonably understood the material. The teacher said she had acquired some new ideas and I smugly returned to my office to view my triumph on tape.

But wait. Midway through the tape, the student camera operator panned in on another student, who was flashing gang symbols. This activity went on for more than a full minute and it was obvious that the two of them were having great fun. The sad part was that I, the great model instructor, was completely oblivious to what was going on. I was in my own little world as I wrote on the chalkboard and spoke more to those who were listening to me. I didn't have a clue as to what was happening with the other students.

The moral of the story is that, contrary to personal belief, I was not quite as good as I thought I was. The problem was mine and I was in need of improvement. Yes, students were misbehaving, but, at the very least, I should have known what was going on in the room and attempted to refocus their energies.

Incidentally, the videotape also vividly portrayed the bald spot on the back of my head—the first time that I was aware of such. Not a real banner day, huh?

Origin

A typical preliminary objective is a reaction to a problem. Inadequate budgets, unsupportive principals, misbehaving children, heavy workloads, poor facilities, and demanding teachers are common problems that call for some type of response.

If readers of this book are similar to most of humanity, their first responses fall in the off-the-top-of-their-heads category. Not having thought it out, they react to the basic problem in the "I need" form, that is, I need more money, I need a supportive principal, I need better-behaving children, I need less work, I need better facilities, and I need understanding teachers.

That's an acceptable place to start.

Upping the Level

Initial reactions need to simmer for a time to allow the brain to rationalize itself anew. Emotions color judgments. The best preliminary objectives move from passionate reaction to dispassionate thought; they depend upon thoughtful observation and analysis.

Sample Objectives

The following examples of preliminary objectives match their higher-order counterparts. Notice that the changes demonstrate the movement of the preliminary objectives from emotional to rational levels. They also assume more personal ownership of the problem statements.

"I need more money" can become "How can I create more resources?"

"I need a supportive principal" can become "How can I garner more support from my principal?"

"I need to protect my library" can become "How can I show the connection between good libraries and good student achievement?"

"I need better-behaving children" can become "How can I promote better behavior in children attending my library media center?"

"I need less work" can become "How can I better manage my workload?" or "How can I gain more personnel support for my library media center?"

"I need a better facility" can become "How can I improve my library media center facility?"

"I need more understanding teachers" can become "How can I work better with the teachers in my school?"

Case Study Introduction

Case studies will illustrate the components of planning detailed in the remaining chapters of Part II. I hope that the stories of Alan Reed and Terri Sanchez will instruct and entertain as each chapter unfolds.

Case Studies

Alan Reed

Alan Reed was a half-time librarian and half-time reading teacher in a small school in the Midwest. Known for his work ethic, he typically arrived at the school at 6:00 a.m. and didn't leave until after 6:00 p.m. Twelve hours a day were necessary to keep up with his duties in both positions. Because Alan was young and single and enjoyed his work, he didn't feel particularly burdened with such a schedule. Of course, as with all educators, he was frequently called upon to attend evening meetings, which added to his hours.

Two years into this job, Alan married Julie and life became even better. But he discovered an important principle—good marriages take time. Although a very understanding person, Julie wanted to enjoy breakfast and dinner conversation and make those small, frequent connections that can mean so much to a successful marriage.

Alan's dilemma was obvious, as was his preliminary objective. He needed more time at home. This was his starting point.

He let it simmer for a while. He talked to Julie about it. He talked to a trusted friend and co-worker about it. He thought about the issues involved. One major issue was that he liked his job, school, and community. He wanted to stay. He also wanted tenure and he didn't want to rock the boat with his principal, who, by the way, was also known for his work ethic. In fact, upon arrival at school every morning, Alan generally found his principal already at work.

Alan had identified needing more time at home as his preliminary objective but he wanted a higher-order objective. His initial contemplation and conversation led him to that next level. He identified his new and improved preliminary objective—to examine his own work practices with a view toward better managing his time.

Terri Sanchez

Terri Sanchez faced a different challenge.

Loaded with personality, Terri had a quick wit and ready smile that could capture the heart of the most reluctant student or teacher. Always willing to help, she was seemingly everywhere at once; her passion for life was always on the surface.

Her inner-city library media center was the envy of other schools. Everyone entering its portals immediately felt the energy and warmth exuded by Terri and by those who worked with her. Not daunted by the problems of her students, she found ways to invite them to enter the world of books and knowledge. In fact, Terri was a central reason for the success of many of the school's tougher youth.

Life was good. Terri was accomplishing her mission. The school was stable—that is, until Dr. Rayburn arrived.

Rayburn had been hired to fix things.

Dismal test scores, crumbling facilities, and deteriorating learning environments at all the district schools had been sensationalized by a media hungry for controversy. As is usually the case in such situations, there was little debate relative to the responsibility of society for this state of affairs. Fingers pointed directly at schools and their leadership. Political solutions soon became the order of the day. Unable to withstand the pressure, the school board was overpowered by state and city politicians, and Mr. Management was appointed the new chief executive.

The change was felt from day one with higher expectations and the threat of termination facing low producers. The principles of business would save the day. Student achievement was the bottom line and nothing would get in the way of it.

Rayburn was hired to promote the new philosophy at Terri's school—and he was a willing participant. He first assembled the staff and told them his mission. He explained that, due to cost efficiencies, any person or program not directly contributing to student achievement would be dismissed or discontinued. He then stated that he would like to meet with the school's librarian as soon as possible, turned on his heel, and strode off. Rayburn's tone and manner warned Terri that trouble lay ahead.

Terri's first thought was instinctive. She must protect her library. A few more moments of reflection gave her a better preliminary objective. She must somehow convince her new boss of the connection between good libraries and good student achievement. Her upcoming meeting would set the stage for all that lay ahead.

Summary

In this chapter, readers see that Alan's disposition prompts him to choose a path of reflection versus confrontation. He takes ownership of his problem. He develops a preliminary objective and then improves it. Terri is in a situation fraught with turmoil and anxiety. External events are creating a crisis of unknown proportion. Her next moves are crucial.

Keep on reading to follow the sagas of Alan and Julie Reed, the young Midwestern couple struggling to find balance between home and work, and of Terri Sanchez, the inner-city library media specialist faced with crisis.

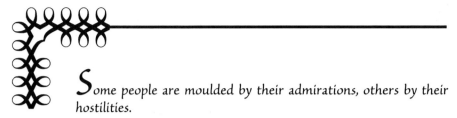

Some people are moulded by their admirations, others by their hostilities.

Elizabeth Bowen

Gathering Intelligence

Politics—the art of pursuing an agenda through people— is inherent to life. Everyone forges relationships that lead to some sort of conclusion. Successful marriages are certainly political alliances. So are jobs. Those who succeed in business most often do so because of their people skills, their abilities to create relationships that garner the best results.

Politics enter into dealing for a used car, choosing a line at the grocery store, even checking out a book from the library. The human brain constantly sifts through a variety of information to make decisions regarding who is honest and who is not, who has a friendly face, and who will treat others with respect. The salesperson, checkout clerk, and librarian consciously and subconsciously choose behavior patterns that lead consumers to certain conclusions.

Most preliminary objectives focus on influencing people. Winning support from administrators, developing resources, and working with teachers and students involve people. Without people, goals and objectives are unattainable; people make things happen.

If this is the case, the most successful library media teachers work best with and through people. They forge lasting relationships, know their students, their teachers, and their administrators, as well as all the subtle nuances of their personalities and backgrounds. They take the time to study the issues and correlate them to the people with whom they work.

Knowing Administrators

In military scenarios, knowing the enemy is paramount. The more the enemy's capabilities, resources, and plans are understood, the more likely the chance of victory over that enemy. The reasons are obvious: the victor usually controls the type, timing, and location of battles. Control is dependent on knowledge. Knowledge is power.

Although I am reluctant to frame school administrators as the enemy, there is still a certain attraction in drawing attention to the parallels. Professional librarians who control their environments and issues know their administrators. The following discussion points out areas of knowledge and study that might prove useful to librarians.

Personal Backgrounds

Things and people are not always what they seem. (Or, as some say, "You can't judge a book by its cover.") The sternest, most autocratic demeanor may camouflage something much softer. The perpetual optimist may suffer grievous personal and family challenges.

The personal backgrounds of school administrators largely shape their professional lives. Their places of birth and circumstances of childhood can affect their speech and reactions.

Where they went to college can make a difference. Their participation in sports or activities, their economic levels, and who
their spouses are can help predict their responses to professional
issues. Military service is an important predictor. Current family
situations—marriage status, problems with children, health of
family members—have a tremendous impact on professional
performance.

Discerning co-workers can pick up clues about someone's
personal background through simple observation and by listening more than by talking. Focused questions in idle workroom-
type conversations can draw out information. "Where were you
raised, Joe?" can elicit more full-blown responses.

It can be useful to know about hobbies, favorite literature,
magazines, movies, and other interests (see Figure 9.1, pages
68–69). Some librarians use this knowledge to advantage by
providing VIP services to administrators along their lines of
interest. Newly purchased books of interest go to them first, as
do the latest editions of their favorite magazines and journals.

The inevitable critics of life may call this "schmoozing" or
"kissing up." Mature librarians do not give these critics a second
thought. Honest, sincere efforts to serve all patrons—including
administrators—can yield great results. It is just good politics.

Few administrators can resist an invitation to lunch. Consider this language: "Joe, I'd really like to get to know you a little
better. How about letting me buy you lunch next Thursday?"
Not only does this strategy create an opportunity for more
knowledge, but it builds relationships and trust, too. Administrators who know something of the personal lives of their staff
members generally feel more ownership toward them—a significant side benefit.

A caution—study and observation don't imply stalking.
Contrary to the tone of some of the language of this book, getting
to know the administrator is *not* a military operation. Administrators are not the enemy, and it's inappropriate to hire private
detectives and set up observation posts.

Intelligence-Gathering Checklist

Personal Background

Birthplace:

Size of family growing up:

Size of family now:

Location and occupation of children if grown:

Unique family circumstances:

Hobbies:

Favorite literature:

Favorite magazines:

Favorite type of movie:

Other interests:

Professional Background

College(s) attended:

Major(s):

Degree(s):

Teaching experience:

Extracurricular sponsorships:

(continued)

Figure 9.1   Intelligence-gathering checklist.

Administrative experience:

Honors:

Publications:

Other special accomplishments:

Professional Goals

School:

Career:

Ancillary:

Leadership Style(s)—circle those that apply

introvert	extrovert	explorer pioneer	settler
left-brained	right-brained	concrete-	abstract-
promoter	controller	analyzer	supporter

Learning Style—visual, auditory, or must learn by doing?

Strategies that I can use as a result of the above data:

Figure 9.1—*Continued.*

I advocate thoughtful, appropriate analysis of the personal background of an administrator with an eye toward the impact of that background on his or her professional personality.

Professional Backgrounds

"There are old administrators and there are bold administrators, but there are very few old, bold administrators." The age and professional backgrounds of administrators make a huge difference in how they respond to their jobs. As pointed out earlier, advancing age can bring wisdom, caution, and sometimes an avoidance of change. Youth can bring impulsiveness and vigor.

Discerning librarians will want to know where their administrators went to college, their major area(s) of study, where they have taught, what extracurricular activities they sponsor, articles they have written (or other special accomplishments), and facts about their administrative careers. Again, lunch, coffee breaks, and casual, focused conversation can elicit this information.

Professional Goals

All administrators have goals, whether productive or nonproductive. Although some goals may seem more reflective of a personal desire to make as few "waves" as possible or even seemingly to do as little as possible, most administrators embrace professional goals that work toward improving levels of service to students, parents, and communities.

A figure-skating analogy may work here. Few things please the eye more than a pair of figure skaters competing in world dance competition. Granted, their overarching goal is to win the competition. Achieving that goal, however, depends upon the artful execution of a series of choreographed moves. Each skater must not only know the moves of the other but must anticipate the timing and subtle nuances of those moves. When the skaters work and flow and move together, they make art. When they don't, they jar the senses.

Librarians who know the goals of their administrators understand and anticipate their decisions. Librarians may not agree with administrators' decisions, but they are better equipped to shape and guide where they can.

Administrators who work with their staffs—and who understand the critical importance of libraries to student achievement—should be cherished. Great things happen when goals match and everyone dances together. They win the gold.

Leadership Styles

"My administrator is a pioneer. She likes to build and then move on."

"Mine is a settler. He may not be flashy, but he is consistent and stable."

"My principal is a controller. She has to know everything about what I'm doing."

"Mine is a promoter. He talks a great game but has trouble with follow-through."

"My administrator is abstract-random and can never make a meeting on time."

"Mine is concrete-sequential and as linear as they come. You know what that means!"

The list could go on and on. The point is that all administrators—and librarians—employ variations and combinations of leadership styles that affect how they view and work in their respective domains. Analysis of leadership style can give librarians real advantage in shaping the reactions and decisions of their administrators.

For example, it is well known that "controlling" administrators like to know the details. They like to participate in planning meetings. They want to be informed and don't like surprises. Librarians who suspect their administrators of this leadership style may want to ask them a few questions to confirm their suspicions: "This is the goal that I'm working toward; does that match your expectations? How much would you like to be involved in the planning process? Would you prefer written or verbal, formal or informal progress reports?"

A librarian can shape an administrator known for creating rapid change by letting him or her know what changes are already in process in the library media center and the status of current goals and programs. It wouldn't hurt to give the administrator a formal briefing on all the functions of the media center; be candid about new programs that will most likely require additional personnel.

Professional librarians must decide, too, whether or not to match their leadership styles with those of their administrators. If the leadership styles generate conflict, the best option may be to keep a low profile and wait for the inevitable change in administration; if they are in tune, the librarian can make substantive progress, or, in rural parlance, make hay while the sun shines!

One caveat—do not assume that people operate under only one leadership style. Most combine at least two styles and maybe more, their use determined by personalities, circumstances, and events.

Learning Styles

Just as we all employ varied leadership styles, so do we all learn in different ways. Some of us learn better by hearing, some by reading, and all of us by doing. An interesting phenomenon is the assumption that other people learn the same way we do. This author happens to learn more by seeing something in print and is always bewildered when board members or teachers don't respond well to the printed word and, instead, prefer oral communications.

The "doing" part presents the greatest challenge. How does one persuade an administrator to learn more about libraries through a useful, hands-on experience? One technique is to invite the administrator to participate in a presentation highlighting some aspect of administrator and librarian cooperation in improving library media centers. School principals generally seek positive recognition and they like seeing their name in lights. A day of rejuvenation at an out-of-town conference doesn't hurt, either; the formal and informal time spent together on such a project can yield significant results. Again, building relationships and trust is key. Possible titles for presentations include:

Librarians and Principals Working Together—Fact or Fantasy?

Librarians and Principals Working Together—An Unbeatable Team.

Creating Resources for Library Media Centers—A Double Dose of Wisdom Needed.

Improving Student Achievement Takes Good Librarians and Good Principals.

Principled Principals—Critical to Media Center Success.

Other techniques include inviting building principals to read to elementary children—a special "principal's chair" could be provided—and/or helping with secondary research projects. It never hurts to invite the press when this occurs; principals are always on the lookout to highlight their schools positively.

Summary

Credible, reliable data drive the best decisions. Library media teachers who expend the time and effort necessary to learn about the personal and professional backgrounds of their administrators can use this information to shape their own futures. Sometimes the information is not readily available and researchers may have to rely more on judgments born of experience—and even instinct.

Now that readers are well versed in intelligence gathering, let's return to our two case studies.

Case Studies

Alan Reed

Alan likes his job but he recognizes the importance of spending time with his new wife. He wants to examine his own work practices to see if he can better manage his time. Although he knows that he may sometime need to discuss his goal with his principal, he is more interested now in seeing whether he can resolve his own problem. This necessarily entails studying himself. Here's how he went about it.

First, he thought about his personal background and how that may be affecting his work. Because Julie was now an important part of his life, he contemplated her personal background as well. In this case, Alan liked what he saw. Julie was outgoing and enjoyed her job as a bank teller. She also enjoyed working with kids and he wondered if there might be ways to include her in some of his school activities; this could give them some more time together, too.

Alan's examination of his professional background didn't yield anything significant. He did wonder, though, if taking a class or seminar on time management might help him.

His professional goals made him think a little more. He tried to determine where he would like to be in his career five years ahead, then ten years ahead. He thought about moving toward an administrative position, but discarded that idea. He wanted more time with his wife and future family, not less. He thought about trying his hand at larger schools and perhaps seeking a library administrator position. That one went by the wayside, too, when he reflected on his enjoyment of rural living. He decided that he wanted to stay right where he was and maybe try writing journal articles or even books someday.

Analysis of his own leadership style revealed even more. After taking several commercially produced inventories, he saw that he tended toward introversion. He also analyzed and thought more critically than most.

As for his learning style, he was definitely a visual learner.

Throughout this self-examination, he couldn't help but consider Julie's characteristics as well. He decided that he needed to talk to her about her professional and personal goals. He realized that she was more extroverted than he and that she was more of a promoter. Alan also noted that Julie was more of an auditory learner—no wonder his love letters hadn't made much of an impression!

Terri Sanchez

Terri Sanchez was in turmoil. Normally optimistic and enthusiastic, she could sense a dark cloud hovering overhead. She had precious little time in which to gather intelligence before her meeting with Dr. Rayburn; she pored over the scant details she had picked up in the last couple of days.

She knew by way of the grapevine that Rayburn was divorced and had children who were grown and living elsewhere. Tall and lean, he had the look of an athlete. His vocabulary belied some past association with the military. "Getting up the hill" was a phrase he had used more than once.

Terri knew that Rayburn had been an administrator in an out-of-state school but not much else about his professional life. Rumor had it that he had worked at the out-of-state school for only a short time. One of Terri's co-workers had noticed a diploma from an Ivy League college hanging on his office wall and remarked that anyone with a doctorate must have some degree of ambition and personal drive. The co-worker also smirked about strong associations between doctorates and egos.

As Dr. Rayburn had stated in his address to staff, his professional goal was to improve student test scores and to eliminate any person or program getting in the way of that goal.

His leadership style was most certainly autocratic and controlling. He was not a salesman; he was most likely concrete-sequential in his approach to problem solving.

Terri desperately needed to know about Rayburn's learning style, but she had little to go on. Most educators with earned doctorates were left-brained and visual learners. She remembered that he had referred to notes during his presentation.

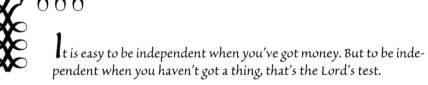

It is easy to be independent when you've got money. But to be independent when you haven't got a thing, that's the Lord's test.

Mahalia Jackson

CHAPTER

10

Resource Analysis and Development

In the United States, there is a disease that is inescapable for most. Although curable, it overtakes millions to the point of no return. It has consumed this generation and threatens the next. Its ravages are seen everywhere. Family breakups, ruined lives, heart failures, burdensome debt, litigious natures, and enriched attorneys all have this disease at their origins.

The name of the disease is greed.

No matter how much we have, we want more. We covet our neighbor's property. We want a better vehicle, a bigger house, a more prestigious job. We are so focused on what we don't have that we fail to remember what we do have. In many cases, we squander our assets. When the newness of something recently acquired wears off, we take the acquisition for granted and it becomes, in our minds, an entitlement instead of a privilege. We neither appreciate it nor take care of it. We are our own worst enemies in this regard.

The focus of this chapter is not the pursuit of more resources, but the recognition, use, and appreciation of those that currently exist.

Available Resources

Professional librarians have at hand myriad resources. These resources—or assets—can be divided into the categories of personnel, budget, fixed assets, and time.

Personnel

By far the most important asset to any library media center, personnel assets include the professional librarian, library assistants, student consumers, parent consumers, teacher consumers, friends of libraries and, yes, even school administrators.

Librarians

Librarians can bring to the table the assets of knowledge, personal drive, compassion, and enthusiasm. They can bring a strong work and service ethic. They can bring a leadership style that influences both staff and students. They can bring experience that will honor past traditions while forging new ones.

Librarians can bring can-do attitudes and creativity. They can bring cheerfulness, style, and grace. They can bring integrity and a sense of loyalty to mission accomplishment.

Neither programs nor money can compensate for a professional librarian dedicated to students and teachers and who possesses, develops, and uses an awesome array of personal assets.

Library Assistants

Library assistants can come in the form of subordinate professional librarians, paraprofessionals, student aides, and citizen volunteers. Each can possess the personal attributes outlined in the preceding paragraphs. Wise librarians nurture these assets and solicit assistants' help, not as individuals used only for the moment and then discarded, but as members of a team.

The reputation of a library media center will, in large part, depend on the word-of-mouth recommendations of its patrons and workers. A business axiom states that it takes longer to gain a reputation than it takes to lose it. Careless, undisciplined words and actions can quickly influence students' and teachers' perceptions of library operations.

Student Consumers

Students are assets. Although educators sometimes joke that they could have a great school if there weren't any students, children and youth nevertheless represent the future of the country. In a few short years, they will be the civic leaders upon whom our generation will depend. They will pay taxes and support our retirements. They will figure out ways to survive and thrive in an increasingly chaotic world.

Library staffs who cherish students and treat them as the leaders of tomorrow guarantee their own success.

Students who are asked for suggestions in creating better library services can make even better resources. They become partners in building the business. Every business (or library media center) must change to meet the needs of its customers; who better to detail those needs than the customers themselves?

Parent Consumers

Parents are most often left out of the loop, especially at the secondary levels. Parents who understand the magic of books and libraries often work wonders with their children; if tapped, they become a valuable resource. Parents can read with their children. They can do their own research and, in the process, exemplify the principles of lifelong learning so vital to this generation. They can spread the word to other parents about the efficacy of self-directed learning and the part that libraries can play in that process.

Smart library staffs find ways to reach out to parents and provide services to them. They enlist parents in volunteer activities, tailor newsletters for them, and provide evening hours. They make phone calls to extend personal invitations. They organize library open houses and perhaps even invite selected parents to lunch. They remember that the list of ways to involve parents is limited only by the creativity of the library staff.

Teacher Consumers

Teachers can be a library staff's most ardent supporters or its worst critics. They influence students' and parents' opinions more than any other constituency. This, alone, is a good enough reason for professional librarians to woo teachers' support.

The more important reason, however, is that solid evidence shows the correlation between good libraries and students' achievements. Libraries that consistently and reliably work with and provide support for teachers strengthen this correlation even more. After all, the school library's central mission is to support the school's academic mission; this cannot be accomplished without the cooperation of teachers.

Again, techniques to reach out to teachers are limited only by the imaginations of library staff members. Personal courtesy goes a long way. Librarians can even ferret out information (see Intelligence-Gathering Checklist, Figure 9.1) relative to personal tastes in literature and journals and forward advance copies to teachers. Yes, teachers are notorious for not returning the materials on time. But the goodwill gained may outweigh the inconveniences. There might even be ways to secure multiple copies so that the teacher may keep one and the library then has one for permanent file.

Instructional support is a huge issue. Savvy library staffs find ways to know what is being taught and work hard to provide supportive materials. Teachers especially appreciate librarians' efforts to work with slow-reading students. Reading invites success in most academic areas; thus, improved reading skills translate directly to improved academic achievement.

Professional librarians want to be cognizant of teachers' leadership and learning styles. Some teachers react better to a personalized, friendly approach. Others may want a get-to-the-point business approach. The best library servants adapt their techniques to the styles and personalities of their teacher consumers.

Friends of Libraries

Friends of Libraries groups can be powerful assets. They raise money for needed projects. They advocate in ways that school employees cannot, for example, by placing just the right phone call to just the right school decision maker at just the right time. They can provide volunteer labor for routine tasks, thereby giving the library staff more time to devote to the academic needs of students and teachers.

Professional librarians who do not have a "Friends" group lack an important resource and should consider forming one. The first step is to secure approval from the appropriate administrator. The next is to find someone to lead the group; this person should have (1) adequate leadership skills, (2) a definite interest in the mission of the library media center and school, and (3) enough available time to be of real help. It helps, too, if the leader happens to be influential in community circles. Once they have identified the right leader, librarians should cultivate a professional friendship with the individual and treat her or him with the same respect a superintendent accords a school board president.

The chosen leader of the Friends group should now be able to guide the rest of the process—finding a good mix of members, identifying goals and objectives, and then accomplishing them.

Library staffs should support (and sometimes shape) the Friends' efforts.

School Administrators

Just like teachers, school administrators can be either great supporters or great detractors. How to cultivate their support is the thesis of this book. Although their mission is to enhance the academic performance of students, school principals suffer from an array of distractions; they are under constant siege from petitioners who believe their issues are the most important in the world—but to a dispassionate observer they can border on the inane. And, as happens to varsity basketball officials, at least half the folks around vocally decry administrators' decisions, and those remaining barely tolerate them.

But that's why they get the big bucks!

Budget

Those who control the purse strings of state budgets frequently lament about educators, "No matter how much we give them, it's never enough. Can they not be satisfied?" It's as if politicians have no concept of what it takes to educate the youth of an increasingly complex and dysfunctional society. More problems and fewer resources are commonplace.

Public educators would be on target if they posted a sign above the doorway of every school that says, "We have done so much for so long with so little that now they expect us to do the impossible with nothing." Well, it may not be quite that bad, but it certainly seems so when budget time comes around.

It does no good, however, for library staffs to hide poorly performing libraries beneath the cloak of inadequate budgets. This ploy only forestalls conversation about the real issues behind poor libraries.

One of those real issues is how the budget is spent. Consider this comparison.

Although personal wealth is often thought to be a function of income, this is not so; it is more a function of saving. Many people have amassed considerable bank accounts on quite average incomes. Contrast that with people who have enjoyed extraordinary incomes but who have little to show for them. The key word is "enjoyed." They lived high, they ate well, they traveled widely, they owned fabulous homes and cars. But, in retrospect, they wasted what they had.

An important business principle is cost efficiency. Those of us at the public trough (I hope you dislike that phrase as much as I do; however, we need to understand the perceptions of our tax-paying publics) can, indeed, never get enough. If we just had this infusion of cash, we could do such and such—a plea heard so often that it is tiresome to everyone. Just like kids with an allowance, we push for more with only passing references to accountability.

By now, readers should feel the extremes of the pendulum. Do we have enough money or don't we? The answers vary as much as the funding levels of each school and library in the United States. The influence of librarians has, in many cases, made the difference between bare subsistence and largess.

Spend well what you have. Make it count. Be accountable. No excuses.

Fixed Assets

Fixed assets are tangible objects; these include furniture, computers, bookshelves, books, and facilities. They are resources that can be used to advantage. Retail stores call this "merchandizing." The arrangement of wares can make a big difference in consumer spending.

Interior decorators, too, make a living by knowing how to please the eye with the content and distribution of the tangible objects of home or office. Even we ordinary mortals try to arrange our humble assets to advantage.

Library staffs who share this talent make a big difference to the learning atmosphere of library media centers.

Because of the difficulty of controlling the size or shape of the facility, most library staffs have to make do with the contents. The amount and kind of contents, however, can be a function of (1) budget, (2) library staff ability to secure donations, (3) library staff ability to beg, borrow, or steal, and (4) the efficacy of the local Friends of Library group.

Time

The last major resource is the great equalizer—time. Everyone owns the same amount and everyone uses it differently; that's the defining point. Some professional librarians are the last to arrive in the morning and the first to leave. One has to wonder whether they are superb organizers, managers, and accomplishers or whether they do just enough to get by. Conversely, some library workers put in extraordinary amounts of time but seem to accomplish little more than their counterparts. Of course, it is always possible that they (1) love to spend every waking minute in the work domain, (2) have real and distressing reasons to avoid their own homes, or (3) are workaholics in a clinical sense.

Successful people find a way to strike a balance; they make the most of their time.

Summary

Professional librarians have resources of personnel, budget, fixed assets, and time. They can maximize their uses and appreciation of these resources by examining each one in detail and including them in any goal setting and plan development processes.

Shall we return to the respective plights of Alan Reed and Terri Sanchez?

Case Studies

Alan Reed

Alan Reed took stock of his resources. He had just read an interesting book that contained a resource checklist and he decided to use it. The first item on the list was personnel.

Alan contemplated the traits and talents that he brought to his school as a librarian. He possessed average knowledge but higher-than-average enthusiasm. He was still learning how to lead. He had integrity and a strong sense of loyalty.

He had no library assistants; this made him think about the possibility of finding a high school student or two who might want to learn about libraries—and provide needed assistance in the process. He could even see about creating an independent-study course about library management that would enable students to earn credit toward graduation. This idea tied in with student consumers. His rural students were generally well mannered and sincere—obvious assets.

He gave more thought to his parent consumers. This was a new idea to him and he liked it. Instinctively, he understood that parents personally connected to his library meant more connections for his students. He would keep that one in mind.

Teacher consumers was an easy category. He was blessed with a great group of teachers. They were mutually supportive and easy to work with. In fact, their personal friendship made him want to serve them even more.

He had several library advocates, although they were not formally organized. Perhaps he could visit with them about his dilemma and seek counsel. He didn't know a whole lot about his principal other than that he was a hard worker, and Alan wanted to do everything to resolve his own situation before he talked to his boss.

Alan's budget and fixed assets were adequate.

But time, now that was the issue. He reviewed once again his work routines and wondered if, in addition to a time-management course, he might ask someone to observe him for a day and offer an opinion as to his efficiency.

Terri Sanchez

Terri's mind was still racing. She, too, had recently read an interesting book that had presented a resource checklist, and even though time was limited, she decided to take a quick mental run-through. What resources did she have?

Number one on her list was confidence. Having been the director of her school's library media center for the last 10 years, she felt she knew her business and could articulate her goals to anyone—even to Dr. Doom (that appellation just popped into her head!). She also knew that her people skills could help. She was a natural salesperson.

Although she had great assistants, they probably couldn't help much in this pressure-cooker, time-sensitive situation. The same applied to her student and parent consumers. This looked like a shoot-out between her and Rayburn.

Her teacher consumers were another matter. Tough, dependable, and loyal, they would provide whatever support they could. They would be her backup plan. If she couldn't prevail in the meeting, she would unleash them. A smile crept upon her face—the first in that hour.

Her library advocacy group could be a part of that backup plan, too—but only if needed. They were strong but it would be preferable to resolve any issues in-house.

Besides, she still wasn't really sure what the issue was; this thought nagged at her again.

Of course, her school administrator was, at this point, the perceived problem. He was not an asset.

Budget and fixed assets were inconsequential to this problem—but maybe that was Rayburn's agenda. Perhaps he just wanted to discuss the budget and ways to reduce it. Terri didn't mind being a team player but didn't want to give away precious dollars lightly.

Time was an unknown. She had to meet shortly but the outcome of the meeting would determine other time constraints.

The Personnel Resources and Assets checklist that follows (see Figure 10.1) can help target areas for special attention. Note the focus on the assets of professional librarians. They are the prime movers of the library media centers.

School Library Media Center Resource Checklist

Personnel Resources and Assets (check appropriate column):

Professional Librarian

	Below Average	Average	Above Average
Knowledge	_____	_____	_____
Personal Drive	_____	_____	_____
Compassion	_____	_____	_____
Enthusiasm	_____	_____	_____
Work Ethic	_____	_____	_____
Leadership	_____	_____	_____
Can-Do Attitude	_____	_____	_____
Creativity	_____	_____	_____
Cheerfulness	_____	_____	_____
Integrity	_____	_____	_____
Style and Grace	_____	_____	_____
Loyalty	_____	_____	_____
Library Assistants	_____	_____	_____
Student Consumers	_____	_____	_____
Parent Consumers	_____	_____	_____
Teacher Consumers	_____	_____	_____
Friends of Libraries	_____	_____	_____
School Administrators	_____	_____	_____

Other Resources and Assets (check which apply):

	Below Average	Average	Above Average
Budget	_____	_____	_____
Fixed Assets	_____	_____	_____
Time	_____	_____	_____

Figure 10.1   School library media center resource checklist.

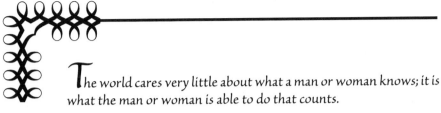

The world cares very little about what a man or woman knows; it is what the man or woman is able to do that counts.

Booker T. Washington

11

Finalizing the Objective

Judith Jeanette Jackson sat hunched over her old wooden desk and stared at the report in front of her. She felt numb and sick as the numbers hammered her brain. Then came the emotions: disbelief, anger, and, finally, resignation.

A fifth-grade teacher in a large southeastern city, Judy—as her friends called her—had given her heart and soul to advancing the academic skills of 28 of the best students that any teacher could ever hope to have. How she enjoyed coming to work each morning and greeting them! All the children were eager to learn and didn't seem to care about the poverty and social challenge that gripped their part of the city.

But the report wasn't good. After nine months of classroom work, these children were still not achieving the "proficiency" level in reading and writing as judged against the standard set several years ago by the state. Judy's mind told her that nine months can't make up for years of societal neglect but, like all good teachers, she had still hoped for victory.

Good scores on this test had been her all-consuming goal for the last year. She had focused every curriculum unit, every lesson plan, and every teaching moment toward this end. Now it was obvious, painfully so, that she had failed. Although her heart said otherwise, her head told her she had not reached the objective, had not accomplished the mission. The children's test scores simply did not measure up and, by extension, neither did she.

Judy straightened the piles on her desk, turned out the light, and locked her door. Head down and deep in thought, she was startled by a soft voice.

"Mrs. Jackson, I was hoping to catch you." The voice belonged to Edith Wilson, the grandmother of Laurie, a shy, slender little girl abandoned by her mother last summer. Emotionally and physically malnourished at the time, Laurie was flourishing under her grandmother's care and, although still behind, had made good academic gains.

Judy often puzzled over Laurie. Seldom participating in normal recess play, Laurie kept to herself and was hard to reach through normal conversation. Judy's attempts to build trust had fetched only quiet smiles.

"What can I do for you, Mrs. Wilson? Is there something wrong with Laurie?" Judy asked.

"No," Edith responded, "I'm just a messenger. Laurie wanted to give you this but she's too shy to do it herself." Edith handed Judy a note, written neatly in pencil on an ordinary piece of school paper.

"Dear Mrs. Jackson," the note began. "I think you are the greatest teacher in the whole world. Thank you for helping me." Judy's eyes filled with tears as she read the ending, "Your friend, Laurie."

Edith continued, "No one knows what this girl has gone through. I don't think we even want to know. But one thing's for sure. She's got a lot of healing to do and, if she's ever going to get well, it's going to be because of people like you. I don't know exactly what you've been doing or what you've been saying, but, whatever it is, please keep doing it. I thank God every day that she has you as her teacher." Edith turned and walked away.

Judy's eyes filled again with tears. Maybe she had, indeed, accomplished her mission. She had just forgotten what it was.

Final Objectives

Final objectives (see Figure 11.1, pages 92–94) should reflect thoughtful contemplation and study. They are more refined than preliminary objectives and are made in consideration of all that is known about the pertinent issues and the resources available.

Good final objectives require strong skills of synthesis—the ability to correlate all the pieces of knowledge and use them in a way that contributes to success. Synthesis requires patience and effort. Again, three minutes of concentration and undivided focus can work wonders.

(Text continues on page 95.)

Final Objective Examples

The lower- and higher-order preliminary objectives given in Chapter 8 are now matched with possible final objectives.

Lower order: I need more money.

Higher order: How can I create more resources?

> Final #1:   To create a Friends of the Library group that will raise funds for library projects.
>
> Final #2:   To prepare three applications for grant funds.
>
> Final #3:   To prepare a budget proposal that reflects reasonable priorities and timelines and present same to my principal at a time most conducive to agreement.

Lower order: I need a supportive principal.

Higher order: How can I garner more support from my principal?

> Final #1:   To document the positive correlation between student test scores and library services.
>
> Final #2:   To create a program of library service that brings positive public recognition to my school.
>
> Final #3:   To build trust with my principal through a variety of professional avenues.

Lower order: I need to protect my library.

Higher order: How can I show the connection between good libraries and student achievement?

> Final #1:   To sponsor an independent study of my library designed to document those activities in my library media center that are directly linked to student achievement.

(continued)

Figure 11.1   Final objective examples.

Final #2: To create a mini-marketing-campaign that highlights the connection between good libraries and student achievement.

Final #3: To survey students and staff regarding what library services they feel are most directly linked to student achievement.

Lower order: I need better-behaving children.

Higher order: How can I promote better behavior in children attending my library media center?

Final #1: To create, with input, reasonable expectations for student library behavior and aggressively adhere to them.

Final #2: To find large, older students, task them with reinforcing the need for library etiquette, and train them in doing same.

Final #3: To create a plan whereby teachers will feel compelledto teach and enforce the rules of library etiquette.

Lower order: I need less work.

Higher order: How can I better manage my workload?

Final #1: To complete formal course work on managing multiple priorities and change any personal habits or patterns that detract from work accomplishment.

Final #2: To create a plan for utilizing outside help—student and parent volunteers.

Final #3: To prioritize work issues and communicate to supervisors those that are relatively unimportant.

Figure 11.1—*Continued.*

Lower order: I need a better facility.

Higher order: How can I improve my library media center facility?

Final #1:   To create a Friends of Library subcommittee that will prepare a viable plan for facility improvement.

Final #2:   To create a student design team for facility improvement.

Final #3:   To create a long-term fund-raising plan for facility improvement.

Lower order: I need more understanding teachers.

Higher order: How can I work better with the teachers in my school?

Final #1:   To create a plan for providing VIP treatment to teachers.

Final #2:   To accomplish at least one extra-mile act of service for a teacher every day.

Final #3:   To prepare a survey (no names required) of teachers that asks for improvement suggestions.

Figure 11.1—*Continued.*

Actual Versus
Intended Outcomes

As Judy's story shows, there can be a difference between actual and intended outcomes. We mere mortals often fail to predict all the possible results of our actions. Just as a pebble thrown into a quiet pond creates ripples, so do our actions create consequences. Many of these unforeseen and unintended consequences are good. Some may not be quite so good.

Planners should peer into their own crystal balls to try to predict all the possible outcomes of their contemplated objectives. Accurate prediction can not only save personal embarrassment but defeat in other ways as well.

Accurate prediction can also shape final objectives and plans in ways not originally contemplated. For example, after a lot of study and thought, a suburban director of library media services, Mr. Smith, established a final objective of building a better professional relationship with his area supervisor. One day, he invited the supervisor to visit his media center. He was showing off some of the new equipment when, to his consternation, two boys squared off and started punching each other. Smith was so angry with this disruption in his plan that he lost control and used racial epithets while breaking up the fight. This caused an even bigger problem for Smith and irreparably damaged his relationship with his boss.

Searching a personal crystal ball necessarily entails reexamination of personal attitudes and should entail consideration of how those attitudes may affect the handling of pressurized situations. Given this knowledge of himself, perhaps Smith's plan would have included contingencies for disruption.

Control

The sagest people save their battles for the most crucial issues. Librarians who feel they must control every outcome of every facet of their professional lives accomplish only partial productivity in their overarching missions. Every moment spent studying and strategizing over trivialities is a moment spent away from serving children.

The flip side of this issue shows that, in some circumstances, a librarian's control is vital to students' achievements.

Personal judgment and common sense determine the difference between the two.

Timing

Timing is everything. Children always assess the moods of their parents and teachers before asking for money or privilege. Politicians gauge the economy prior to raising taxes. School boards must understand the nuances of timing when going after a bond election.

The same holds true for professional librarians seeking support. Knowing "when to hold 'em and when to fold 'em" is a skill worth having. Asking for the moon won't work if trusting relationships do not yet exist between the librarian and her or his principal.

I once had a transportation director who issued the standing offer of a place for me to get away from the daily grind and enjoy a "beer and cigar" with him. Although the beer and cigar never materialized (it was, after all, a school), the get-away place did. This savvy gentleman had gained complete access for (1) building trust, (2) keeping me personally informed of his department's issues, and (3) knowing the proper time to make requests.

Evaluative Components

Final objectives should be developed with evaluation in mind. Goals based on concrete evidence are more readily evaluated than those that are not. In fact, goals based on un- quantified perceptions and emotional responses are seldom use- ful or accomplished.

For example, goals relating to increasing budget alloca- tions, library usage, collections, and so forth, are simple to quan- tify and to evaluate. Planners and doers know when they have met the goals in these areas; they know whether they've been successful or not.

A goal to build stakeholder support is more difficult to quantify and, therefore, to evaluate. But it is possible when effort is applied in determining the evidence of the desired support.

For instance, administrators hang out where they feel com- fortable. Principals who don't spend much time in the library may not feel comfortable there. Librarians can keep statistics about the frequency of the administrator's visits and find ways to increase that frequency. Of course, the librarian must weigh the inconvenience and pressures involved with increased over- sight (surveillance?) against the possibilities of the increased tangible support that can result when administrators familiarize themselves with operations at the library media center.

If the librarian can't evaluate the accomplishment of a pro- posed goal, he or she should seriously consider eliminating it. Anything worth doing is worth being evaluated.

Revenge Motives

Goals to "get even" for alleged grievances are unproductive and indicative of immaturity. They have no place in a profes- sional's repertoire.

Summary

Chapter 8 showed that lower-order preliminary objectives are emotional responses to external events; higher-order preliminary objectives are more rational responses to external events that reflect individual responsibility.

This chapter established final objectives as rational responses to external events that synthesize individual responsibility, all that is known about the issues, resources available, the possibility of unintended consequences, self-discipline and judgment in issues of control and revenge, consideration of the aspects of timing, and evaluative components.

Let's take a quick look at Alan Reed and Terri Sanchez to see how they are progressing in their studies.

Case Studies

Alan Reed

Alan was impressed with the number of available resources that he had not used. High school students could be a great help. So could parents. There was a community college nearby that offered seminars in managing multiple priorities and time management.

He decided he was ready to set a final objective. His lower-order preliminary objective was to spend more time at home. His higher-order objective was better management of his time through examining his own work practices. After study and thought, his final objective centered on increasing his work productivity skills. He kept in the back of his mind, however, the possibility of creating a plan for volunteer support.

Terri Sanchez _____

Terri couldn't decide whether she was more frightened or furious—probably a combination of both. Her meeting with Dr. Rayburn was less than an hour away and her adrenaline was reaching for new heights. Again, she pondered her objectives.

Her lower-order preliminary objective had focused on protecting her library from Rayburn's perceived threat. This had led to her higher-order objective of helping Rayburn understand the connection between good libraries and good student achievement. After her limited, informal research and contemplation time, she settled on her final objective—to prepare a mental plan that would allow her to control this very crucial meeting. The plan would provide her with multiple options designed to counter any predictable scenario.

Terri's confidence rose again as she began jotting down notes.

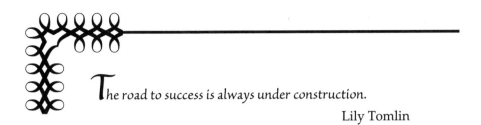

The road to success is always under construction.

Lily Tomlin

The Plan—Strategies and Timelines

We have arrived at last! Developing the plan of strategies and timelines is the most important piece of any quest for greater administrative support. More important, even, than plan implementation. A well-researched, thoughtfully prepared plan (see Figure 12.1, page 102) sets the stage for implementation and can make the critical difference between success and failure. The adage, "When you fail to plan, you plan to fail" is extraordinarily accurate.

A Plan Outline

What
   Final objective
   Intermediate checkpoints
   Overall strategy
   Ancillary strategies

Who
   The planner
   Helpers
   The person of focus

When
   Premeditation versus reaction
   Placement in school year
   Day of week
   Time of day

Where
   Setting

Why
   Quelled or fired-up commitment

Decisions
   Creativity
   Timing
   Approaches

Figure 12.1   A plan outline.

All that has been learned from establishing lower- and higher-order objectives, gathering intelligence, analyzing resources, and setting the final objective goes into establishing the strategies and timelines necessary to accomplish the final objective. Nothing can be left out. No detail is too small for consideration. Experienced planners know that just as writing creates thought, so does the actual detailing of plan components. Each component has the potential to cause serious thinking, which may lead to more intelligence gathering and resource analysis. Final objectives may even be altered or eliminated entirely as judgment and common sense overtake irrationalities that may not have been apparent up to that point.

Plan Components

In common language, plan components provide the details of what, who, when, where, and why. If time allows, they should be organized in outline form and written down. As taught by old Mrs. McGillicuddy in freshman English, the very process of outlining creates questions, which create contemplation; contemplation leads to more study, which leads to a better plan.

Thinking out of the boxes and seeking ideas from others can significantly improve planning. Roger von Oech has written a marvelous book, *A Whack on the Side of the Head*, which is a must-read. It inspires readers to greater creativity and gives useful tips in that vein.

Considerations of timing are critical. Able tacticians pick their battles and their moments. Conductors of respected orchestras know the precise moment to bring in the separate instruments. Conductors of respected libraries enjoy that same instinct; they know just when to make a move and when to hold off.

Approaches are critical, too. Is it better to confront an issue directly—a frontal assault? Or would it be more advantageous to try an end run? Which approach has the best chance for success with a minimum of unintended, negative consequences?

Remember the old saw, "There is more than one way to skin a cat."

The popularity of action shows in the genre of *Mission Impossible* attests to the intellectual and emotional appeal of thorough planning and, of course, its exciting execution. Although the elimination of a despicable villain may be the goal, never do we see a mass of troops storming the main gate in a frontal assault. There are reasons this is so. First, the consequences could come back to haunt friendly powers. Second, it's over too quickly and producers can't fill their 60-minute time slots, complete with riveting commercials.

As an aside, the entire advertising industry is another example of how strategies produce tangible goals!

What

The "what" is the central thesis of the plan, the defining strategy replete with its ancillary strategies. In the jewel heist, it is the contrived entrance, the disabling of security measures, and the elusive getaway. In the unsupportive school principal situation, it could be the information campaign, pressure from allies, and an invitation to join the librarian in a presentation.

Another analogy is mountain climbing. When climbing one of Colorado's 54 "fourteeners" (over 14,000 feet in elevation), the goal is to reach the mountain peak, as well as gaining the privilege of penciling one's name on the list of successful climbers contained in the aluminum cylinder stashed at the top. Special checkpoints—or intermediate objectives—mark the way.

On Mount Blanca in south-central Colorado, one intermediate objective is Lake Como, usually the staging point for the next morning's assault. Another is the beginning of the rock-laced path (this is not a technical climb) that leads to the final ridge. The last intermediate checkpoint is the ridge, 100-plus yards of don't-look-down-either-side until the peak is reached.

Planners looking for increased support from administrators should consider which checkpoints—intermediate objectives—indicate movement toward the final objective. One intermediate objective could be the principal's verbal statement at a faculty meeting of library support. Another could be a written memo or article expressing the same thing. Another could be the principal's critical help with a special library project.

Mountain climbing is about as linear as a plan can get. The goal is to get to the top; there are generally not too many choices in the approach. This may not be the case in library planning. Perhaps a scattergun method would better suit the needs and tastes of the planner. Not all challenges in life are linear—contrary to the thinking of many lead-bottomed administrators!

The overall "what" will include the plan outline containing the intermediate checkpoints. It will then give the "sub-whats" involved in accomplishing each of the intermediate objectives. These pieces may then lead to even more detailed plans as smaller challenges, mini-objectives, emerge.

Again, the more detailed the plan, the better the chance for success.

Who

The most important "who" is the planner. The buck stops with that person. She or he alone is responsible for success or failure. External events may create unanticipated challenge, but thorough planning provides for contingencies. Incidentally, the more thorough the planning, the less likelihood of disruption by external events.

People who are allies and resources are players, too. A mission team may have a leader, but the team members, each with a critical skill, accomplish the plan. Planners are advised to select carefully those who participate. Special "prompting," or even training, may be necessary. A leader is only as good as the members of the team. Allies to professional librarians generally include teachers, friends of libraries, and students.

Depending on the nature of the final objective, another "who" may be the object of the plan. In the action genre example, this would be the despicable villain. In a school setting, it may be the principal. It could be a businessperson of influence or a teacher or student causing the problems. With a plan to reward an outstanding supporter, the "who" would be the person being recognized.

When

The "when" involves experience, common sense, and judgment. Experienced climbers make their final ascents in the morning. A mountain peak is not the best place to be during an afternoon thunderstorm with its accompanying lightning.

Professional librarians also maneuver their way through thunderstorms. They know that sound people skills are valuable tools. Confrontation generally leads to conflagration—someone ends up getting "burned."

However, there may be times when confrontation is the best option for moving someone off dead center. If this is the case, the move should always be premeditated. Angry, spur-of-the-moment reactions can create serious problems. Effective, productive confrontation is planned and executed carefully.

Where

Seemingly inconsequential to some, the location and setting of plan components can make a difference. Consider this.

Mrs. Jones wants to have a serious conversation with her principal (Mr. Busy) about budget needs. She has tried making appointments, but something always gets in the way. She doesn't think Mr. Busy is deliberately avoiding her, it just seems that some crisis or other happens at the exact time of their appointment. The last time the fire alarm was set off by who-knows-which student trying to live up to the reputation of his father.

How can Mrs. Jones proceed? She has thought about catching Mr. Busy on the fly, but is worried that he will be distracted and won't give her his undivided attention. She has considered kidnapping, but can't predict his reaction. Sometimes bosses don't have a sense of humor. What are her options?

After spending three minutes entirely focused on the dilemma, she came up with these alternatives: (1) keep trying the appointment route in the hope that she will eventually get the time she needs, (2) bribe the principal's secretary and ask her to create a good opportunity, or (3) invite the principal to a special breakfast in the library.

Mrs. Jones chose both 2 and 3. She would solicit help from the secretary in finding a before-school time not already blocked out and then create a special event in her library setting. She would find out what Mr. Busy likes to eat for breakfast and then send him a written invitation. At the breakfast, she would remain sensitive to time constraints and seize the appropriate moments to instruct and ask for advice. She would post a sign on the library door advising of the meeting in progress and, just in case there are gossips in the building, she would invite a trusted colleague to share breakfast with them. The colleague could even lend active support in any proposals.

Incidentally, those readers who would accuse Mrs. Jones of blatant "schmoozing" are reminded that diplomacy among governments revolves around such acts of conciliation and kindness. It is a time-honored tradition that leads to better relationships and trust. The first responsibility of any library media center leader is to further the interests of that center. If fixing breakfast for the principal gets the job done, then so be it. Of course, it wouldn't hurt to ask a school service club to help with the breakfast. Students are always a great addition!

The "where" of library plans should usually be the library media center. That is where the action is. When presentations or fund-raisers are being conducted, astute professionals may want to create a display that reminds participants of the library setting. Technology presentations should include images of the library center, replete with images of happy students and teachers.

Why

The "why" can either quell or fire the passion for any contemplated plan. Its placement at the end of the questions is fortuitous. It gives a planner pause to think one more time about the advisability of the plan. Is the plan worth it? Will it create more problems than it solves? What are its chances of success?

It is surprising how many times plan development turns out to be nothing more than catharsis for the soul, therapy for those wounded by unthinking, insensitive administrators or other associates. If this is the outcome, then it is cheap for the price. Professional therapists cost a lot more.

The "why" can also fire passions for seeing the plan through. It reminds the planner of all the reasons the actions need to be taken and motivates action even on days that seem to drag just a bit.

Example

Mr. Nesbitt was a man with a plan. A lifelong servant to kids and teachers, he worked hard to maintain his library with minimal resources. At long last, tired of seeing his library's needs pushed aside by a succession of shortsighted principals, Mr. Nesbitt decided to take action. He created a plan that would be the envy of any master planner. He was determined to put a stop to his library's needs being pushed aside. He went back to that time and time again. It became his private mantra. It kept him going even when the implementation phase encountered problems. He was tired of his library's needs being pushed aside. He was going to do something about it—and he did. Nicely, of course. With grace and dignity and a minimum of confrontation. But he got the job done.

Of course, his plan involved meeting with teachers, selected parents and students, and his principal. In those meetings, he created consensus for acquisitions that included equipment, books, and automation. He sold his need for a budget that was consistent, comprehensive, and adequate for the maintenance of a top-of-the-line library media center.

He put everything in writing and even had a small "sign-ing" party when agreement was reached. Then he spent the next year implementing all the details.

Nesbitt's only regret? He wished that he had had the cour-age to seize the initiative years before that. He was sorry that the "why" had taken him longer than most to realize.

Summary

Developing a well-rounded, thoughtfully prepared plan of strategies and timelines is the most important piece of any quest for greater support from administrators. The components of successful plans provide the details of what, who, when, where, and why.

Thinking out of the boxes can create plans with surpris-ingly effective components. An emphasis on service is key.

Case Studies

So far, Alan and Terri have each done their best to shape events rather than be shaped by them. They have accepted ac-countability and have focused their energies on resolving their situations. They have, to the extent expected by any reasonable, impartial observer, established their objectives and have done their homework. Now they are ready to document their plans.

Alan Reed

Alan looked thoughtfully at Julie over the remains of a late-night snack and said, "I think I'll stay up a bit and put my plan together."

Julie's reaction didn't surprise him. "Would you like me to help?" she offered.

"No, this might take a while. Go ahead and get some sleep."

Julie murmured some encouragement and tactfully withdrew. She sensed Alan's sincerity and need to do some more serious thinking. How grateful she was to have Alan for her life partner. "He really does have potential," she said to herself, confirming anew her feelings toward him.

Alan looked at the blank sheet of paper for just a moment before starting to make notes. After so much study and contemplation, it was exhilarating finally to organize his thoughts into something coherent.

Two hours later, he looked at the clock, went over his outline one more time, and stood up with a satisfied air. He liked what he saw. The strategies and timelines were doable and should help him reach his objective.

Alan's Plan

Final objective:	To increase my work productivity skills.
Overall strategy:	Improve my skills in time management.
Ancillary strategies:	Participate in seminar on time management.
	Participate in seminar on managing multiple priorities.
	Read two books on similar topics.
	Communicate to co-workers the reasons for my quest to improve.
Who:	I will arrange for and attend the seminars.
	I will find the best books and read them.
	I will communicate to co-workers the reasons for my quest.
	I will consult Julie every step of the way.
	I will be sensitive to the reactions of my co-workers.
When:	As soon as the seminars are available; the sooner the better.

	Within the next two weeks to have at least one book read.
	Within a week to start low-key communications to coworkers.
Where:	Local college campus and my own work environment.
Why:	To improve the quality of life for me, Julie, and any future family.

Alan chuckled as he thought about the decision points and their involving creativity, timing, and approaches. The timing and approaches were fairly straightforward. The creativity piece offered a chance for some fun with his staff.

One of the things he was thinking about was preparing an "I love Julie" memo to his coworkers, which would explain his dilemma and his proposed solution. He would ask their advice and establish a mailbox in his library for them to send their words of "advice to the lovelorn." He hoped this strategy would help gain their support for his quest and also generate some more good ideas. He would be very careful to acknowledge his responsibility in carrying his share of the load in the school, but he would also acknowledge his responsibility in establishing a work pattern to support a good family life.

Of course, Alan fleshed out his outline with all the details involved in finding classes and books and in communicating with Julie and his coworkers. The outline even contained some contingencies in the event that his principal was less than thrilled with his approach. Rightly or wrongly (time would tell), he had opted to leave his principal out of the communication loop for the time being. He wanted to try to gain the teachers' support first.

"Repentance is sometimes easier than permission," he thought wryly.

Terri Sanchez

We left Terri hurriedly jotting down notes for her meeting less than an hour away. When she next looked at the clock, only ten minutes remained.

She reflected on where she was. To begin with, the very act of writing down her options and possible strategies had diffused her anger. That was good. Her mind would function much better unfettered by the trappings of emotion. Next, her notes reminded her that Dr. Rayburn's agenda was still a mystery. It was possible that he wanted to discuss something relatively innocuous, although Terri's instincts said otherwise.

Terri's Plan

Final Objective:	To control the outcome of the meeting with Dr. Rayburn.
Overall strategy:	To predict possible scenarios and options for addressing them.
Ancillary strategies:	To stay calm and focused on the needs of her library.
	To use her assets of knowledge and personality.
	To keep service to students her number-one priority.
Possible options:	Rayburn wants to solicit her advice.
	Rayburn wants to cut her budget.
	Rayburn wants to fire her.
	Rayburn wants to give her additional responsibilities.
	Rayburn wants to discuss the continuing role of her library.

All of the above.

None of the above.

Who:	It's all her and Rayburn at this point.
	Reinforcements (co-workers and volunteers) may be needed later.
When:	Now.
Where:	Rayburn's office.
Why:	Her students depend on her professional composure and response.

Terri smoothed her hair, straightened her suit, and walked purposefully toward Dr. Rayburn's office. The secretary ushered her in and Dr. Rayburn rose to greet her.

*O*nce you've done the mental work, there comes a point you have to throw yourself into the action and put your heart on the line. That means not only being brave, but being passionate toward yourself, your teammates and your opponents.

Phil Jackson

Implementing the Plan

Coach Jaworski had a problem. Newly hired as the varsity basketball coach, he had been given a teaching assignment at one of the feeder middle schools. That was fine but, after only three days on the job, he was ready to quit. From the first day, it was apparent that he was not cut out to teach youth whose sole ambition was the destruction of his teaching career.

His students were horrible in every sense of the word. They were undisciplined little monsters without any saving graces that he could see. They refused to participate in class work, spent most of their time talking and passing notes, and were obviously in complete control of him. His 250-pound frame shuddered to think how he was going to survive the year.

This situation was contrary to the plan he had envisioned. He knew he needed help and he needed it fast. He decided to visit the teacher next door after school. Although quiet, she looked friendly enough.

Her name was Ms. Dinsmore. She looked younger than her 28 years, her prettier-than-average face framed by large eyeglasses. She had a slight build and a soft voice. Coach Jaworski's first thought was one of disdain. "How could she possibly help me," he mused; "she can't weigh over 95 pounds!" But he was intrigued by the relative quiet in her class.

After hearing the coach's plea, Ms. Dinsmore agreed to step into his classroom and give him a pointer or two when things got out of hand.

It didn't take long. Ten minutes into the next period, two boys interrupted their loud banter to sail some wadded-up trash in the direction of the coach while the other monsters just laughed. Chaos revisited.

No one noticed the slender figure of Ms. Dinsmore until she stood right next to the offenders. She placed her hand lightly on the shoulder of the nearest, looked right into the eyes of the other and said in a friendly tone just barely edged with steel, "I think it's time you boys sat down." They sat down. Then she turned to the rest of the class and suggested that they open their books. They opened their books. When all was quiet, she looked at Coach Jaworski and said demurely, "They're all yours, Coach. Let me know if anyone gets out of hand."

Leadership

The above illustrates one of the fascinating aspects of leadership—leaders come in every shape and size (for a leadership checklist, see Figure 13.1). Some are blustery. Some are not. Some are smart. Some are not. It is surprising how many 250-pound coaches freeze at the thought of managing middle-school kids. It is equally surprising how small, quiet teachers can command attention and respect from the same children.

Leadership Checklist

	Below Average	Average	Above Average
I rate myself. . .			
Charisma	_____	_____	_____
Confidence	_____	_____	_____
Credibility	_____	_____	_____
Perseverance	_____	_____	_____
People Skills	_____	_____	_____
Proficiency	_____	_____	_____
Self-Improvement	_____	_____	_____
Caring	_____	_____	_____
Communication	_____	_____	_____
Example	_____	_____	_____
Delegation	_____	_____	_____
Team-Sense	_____	_____	_____
Judgment	_____	_____	_____
Initiative	_____	_____	_____
Authority	_____	_____	_____
Intensity	_____	_____	_____
Enthusiasm	_____	_____	_____

Area most in need of improvement:

Plan for personal improvement:

Figure 13.1   Leadership checklist.

That mystical, magical trait called "charisma" is elusive. Although inherent in many of the great leaders in our past and present, it is not essential. Good leaders find their own formulas for success. What was it about Ms. Dinsmore that fostered her effectiveness? She obviously had a sense of confidence and the kids felt that. She was on her own turf too, very comfortable with the requirements and status of her position. Coach Jaworski was more comfortable on the basketball court than in a middle-school classroom.

Leadership has been defined as "getting the job done by bringing out the best in people." This definition directly applies to plan implementation because the qualities of leadership are the same qualities needed to carry out any plan successfully. Credibility, perseverance, people skills, judgment, and charisma are useful ingredients. So is enthusiasm. As noted before, every-one searches for a formula that works. The endless variations to those formulas may work for one but not for another.

Just for the sake of doing something different, let's exam-ine the traits of leadership espoused by the armed forces. Of all organizations, they have the longest track record—over 200 years—of leadership and have made its study a requirement for advancement. This examination will not only instruct in tech-niques of leadership and accomplishing plans, but it may give more insight into the psyches of some school administrators.

The following 10 principles can admonish or counsel; the language has been adapted to align to the education profession. Insightful readers will note that the precepts could just as easily represent the thinking of a Fortune 500, governmental, or any other entity leader. The principles are the same.

Proficiency

Be technically and tactically proficient. This refers to creating a sound plan and then following it in a way that allows for contingencies and insists upon success. It is similar to a coach who studies his or her game incessantly and can compete strate-gically with anyone. It is similar to a professional librarian who knows the business backward and forward and who is constantly learning.

Tactical proficiency implies knowledge about human nature and reflects good intelligence-gathering. People skills are paramount. Knowing when to plead or when to scold and how to do each in a manner that contributes to goal accomplishment is part of tactical proficiency.

Self-Improvement

Know yourself and seek self-improvement. Credibility is the key issue here. Those trying to pursue a plan that involves influencing people must, themselves, be credible. Most plans seek to improve some situation and they ask people to change some aspect of their thinking or performance. To seek change in others while refusing to acknowledge the need for personal change or improvement is folly.

Accurate judgment concerning one's own strengths and limitations is the first step toward self-improvement. The biblical admonition to behold the "beam" in our own eye before searching for the "mote" in another's eye applies here too.

It could prove worthwhile at this point to read Chapter 2 again. (It's the one that lists different personality descriptors and encourages self-evaluation.)

Caring

Know your co-workers and look out for their welfare. Service and kindness are reciprocal. Those who take care of others will be taken care of by others. Those who are tolerant of others are more likely to be tolerated by others. This is the "what goes around, comes around" rule.

Plan implementers frequently encounter unforeseen pitfalls in their pursuit of goal accomplishment, and friendly and tolerant co-workers can make a difference in how obstacles are handled and overcome.

Another time-tested adage applies here: "People won't care how much you know until they know how much you care."

Communication

Keep your co-workers informed. We live in an information age. Those who don't share needed information are perceived as aloof, uncaring, and not part of the team. People are more willing to help when they understand reasons. Timely and appropriate communication is a critical factor of success.

Inappropriate communication includes the tendency of education family members to spread gossip and unfair judgments about others; this is destructive behavior and serves no positive purpose.

Example

Set the example. Who we are speaks louder than what we say. Personal credibility is again at stake with this precept. The "I-take-five-coffee-breaks-a-day" principal who makes sweeping pronouncements about teachers beating the kids out the door at the end of the day quickly gains a reputation for hypocrisy. So does the gossipy librarian who criticizes a boss for spreading rumors.

Self-discipline is the best example to set. When we were young, our mothers told us when we were out of line. Then our teachers took over. Some of us had drill instructors or trusted mentors who gave us even more help. But there is seldom anyone to tell us old-timers when we need to correct some aspect of our lives. That's why it is so important to evaluate ourselves and take action to improve where needed.

People who exercise discipline in judgment, comments, and actions contribute great things to society. They are credible.

Delegation

Ensure that the task is understood, supervised, and accomplished. Most plans consist of many small pieces. Some may be documented, some may not. They are all important. A professional librarian who makes sure that every delegated task is completely understood and supervised appropriately will accomplish tasks successfully.

Some employees need more supervision than others. This is a part of knowing co-workers and their strengths and limitations. Some supervising librarians are natural "controllers" and need to back off a little. Because people grow through mistakes, sometimes the growth and development of a staff member is more important than the expected task accomplishment.

This principle implies calls for plan implementers to communicate the importance and process of the plan to those who may play some role in its accomplishment.

Team Sense

Develop a team. Synergism describes a situation where two or more parts combine to create an effect that a single part acting on its own is incapable of producing; that is, the whole is greater than the sum of its parts. The best teams are synergistic. Effective leaders and plan implementers know this and use it to advantage.

Everyone wants to be part of a winning team. Team spirit is fostered by environment and follow-through. Librarians who talk about teams with respect and enthusiasm and who recognize the potential in team members establish a fertile environment. They provide formal and informal settings for teamwork and dialogue. They reward success in any conceivable way.

Developing a sense of responsibility in team members forges another link to success. Effective delegation of assignments and appropriate supervision help in this regard. But the truly great teams depend on those creative, enthusiastic people who live by the carpe diem code; their ardor and verve inspire everyone to seize the day.

Judgment

Make sound and timely decisions. Good decision making comes from good data. It also comes from appropriately balanced considerations of the heart and the mind. Compassionate analysis—or analytic compassion—can aid decision making.

Good decisions rely on analysis of consequences, the ripple effects particular decisions create. A decision maker who takes the time to think through all possible consequences gains an edge in shaping plans, making those minor course corrections so critical to the plan's outcome.

Initiative

Seek responsibility and take responsibility for actions. Self-starters are frequently the most valued employees. They take the initiative and make things happen. They take risks. They think, study, plan, and devote their entire beings to accomplishing the task. Then they hold themselves accountable for success.

Professional librarians with these traits are like gold. Their credibility is generally so strong that major plans to develop support for their library media centers are not necessary. They already have the support. Their planning is more oriented toward increasing curriculum coordination or creating new services. It is higher order; it reaches beyond the basics.

Of all the leadership traits, responsibility tells the most about the abilities of a plan implementer.

Authority

Employ your authority in accordance with its capabilities. Ego and pride have been the downfall of many. It happens all too often that quiet, willing workers promoted to positions of responsibility turn into the worst caricatures of themselves—proud, willful authoritarians who brook no opposition and think themselves above the rules of human decency. Unfortunately, too many administrators have acquired this disease. But they are not the only ones. Even professional librarians have been known to edge in this direction.

Real authority comes from the skills of persuasion and the force of reason. People in this category get the job done by bringing out the best in people. They are the most effective leaders and plan implementers.

Two More: Intensity and Enthusiasm

Although implied in the above, intensity and enthusiasm are two more leadership traits that bear emphasis.

After umpteen years in the education business, I've found that the one thing separating great teachers from the merely good ones is intensity. Great teachers insist that students learn. They won't accept anything less than the best efforts of themselves, their students, and even parents of students. They don't punch a clock. They work until the job is done. If Johnny hasn't learned what he should have during the regular school day, then Johnny stays after school to catch up. And woe be unto the parent who complains. These extraordinary teachers set the tone at the beginning of the year with students and parents; everyone knows from the outset that much will be expected and much will be learned.

Intensity doesn't necessarily mean crankiness. Our changing times are mandating softer approaches to dealing with a society used to instant gratification and litigation. Today's intensity requires more of an iron fist in a velvet glove.

Library media specialists who are intense about accomplishment and bringing out the best in people will enjoy success.

Enthusiasm is the glue that binds, a strong catalyst for accomplishment. Enthusiasm builds teams, bridges gaps, inspires innovation, and makes life a whole lot more fun. The following example may sound a bit extreme, but it really happened and it graphically portrays the principle of enthusiasm in an unexpected way.

My daughter, the high school cross-country star, was once playing a late-night game of hide-and-go-seek with her friends on a nearby campus. Running full tilt, she rushed around the corner of a large building and saw too late the plate glass window looming directly ahead. Realizing that she couldn't stop, she covered her face with her hands and plowed into the window with enough force to carry her through it and into the building. In other words, she hit that window with enthusiasm! And that enthusiasm probably saved the day. Tremendously fortunate, she suffered only the most minor scratches and cuts. If she had hesitated, she would have gotten hung up in the glass and suffered serious injury.

Many of life's barriers can be overcome with enthusiasm.

Summary

Charisma, confidence, credibility, perseverance, people skills, proficiency, self-improvement, caring, communication, example, delegation, team sense, judgment, initiative, authority, intensity, and enthusiasm are all personal attributes that can be mixed and matched in unending variety to create individual formulas for successful plan implementation.

Case Studies

Alan Reed and Terri Sanchez are eagerly waiting to finish their stories. Separated by gender, setting, and circumstance, their challenges point out the complexity of life's situations. Everyone's challenges are just different enough to ensure that there is no one-size-fits-all solution.

Alan Reed

Alan almost laughed out loud. He had just spent the entire weekend away from his beloved wife, Julie, learning "how to have more time with loved ones." Although the time-management seminar had been instructive, it did seem ironic.

The books that he had been reading were informative, too. One theme kept recurring in both the seminar and the literature: the need for a daily plan. Alan tried it and found that a things-to-do list helped him focus on what needed to be done and kept him on track in getting it done.

Before, any person or project that happened to intrude on his day had distracted him. Now, his few moments of planning allowed him to select priorities. It was amazing just how much difference it made. "The human mind is remarkable," he thought. "Almost subconsciously, it creates a path to a destination. It just has to know what the destination is."

As it was turning out, the accomplishment of his plan was proceeding smoothly. The "advice for the lovelorn" idea had worked and he was getting some good ideas from his peers. One teacher's response was particularly thoughtful.

"Dear Lovelorn," the teacher wrote. "After 20 years I can still say that I picked the right profession. Working with the future of humanity is tremendously rewarding. However, 20 years have also taught me that my most important work is with my own family. You're on the right track. Figure out now how to do that. No one has ever looked back at life and said, 'I wish that I had spent more time in the office.' "

An unexpected by-product was the involvement of his students. They really liked the "lovelorn" box and submitted ideas that reflected their own lives. "My mom and dad aren't together anymore," said one young girl. "I know it sounds old-fashioned, but I think they would still be if they had gone on fun dates together."

Alan sat for a moment contemplating his day. It was five o'clock and the library was quiet. He was satisfied with the way things were going, but one thought kept nagging at him. He had been avoiding his principal and he didn't feel good about that. It was silly, really. It was almost as though he didn't want to tell his father what he had been up to. "Grow up," he said to himself. "It's not that big of a deal. I'll talk to him tomorrow."

He got up and was turning for the light switch when he heard a voice behind him.

It was his principal.

Terri Sanchez

Dr. Rayburn looked Terri straight in the eye. "It's not my style to beat around the bush," he said, "so I'll get straight to the point. Our school is in trouble. Test scores are in the cellar. Enrollment is down. We've got teachers who aren't pulling their weight. I've been hired to fix that. I'm told that you are one of the few bright spots here and I'd like your help."

Terri fished for more information. She still wasn't sure of Rayburn's agenda. "What would you like me to do?" she asked.

"I want you to be my eyes and ears in this building. I need to know everything that is going on, who is saying what, who is doing what. I need help in knowing which teachers to get rid of and which ones to keep. I need good information and you can get it for me. I know it will be hard, but it would probably be the most valuable service you could ever do for our kids." Rayburn hesitated and looked expectantly at Terri.

He wants me to rat on my teachers, my friends, Terri thought. *This guy's out of his mind.*

"One more thing," Rayburn said. "If you'll be my partner in this, I am empowered to offer you a bonus that will make it worth your while."

This was insanity. None of Terri's possible scenarios even remotely connected with Rayburn's agenda. Her mind whirled, dancing around every thought of the last two hours. She searched for common ground. The only commonality was children. Rayburn had mentioned service to kids.

Terri needed to respond. But she knew that her first words would set the tone for everything to come. She couldn't let her emotions get in the way. She was, in effect, representing everything good about her school and her peers and she had to somehow lead Rayburn in a different direction. Once that was done, she could figure out the best way to deal with his appalling lack of integrity and pitiful attempt at bribery.

"Dr. Rayburn," she began cautiously, "I am flattered that you think enough of me to seek my help. I have loved this school and those within it for many years now." The words started coming faster now. She knew what direction to take.

"It is true that things are bad here. Our kids and teachers have it really rough. Life hasn't been fair to any of us. We all know that whining about our problems doesn't help, but we can't seem to get beyond that stage. Perhaps that's the reason you've been sent here. We need your help."

Rayburn leaned forward. He was interested.

"And there's something you could do that would make more difference for our teachers and kids than anything else," she continued. "You could tell us what your bottom-line goal is for our school. Make it just one thing. If it's student behavior, tell us what evidence would convince you that behavior has improved to your expectation. If it's test scores, tell us what test and what score you would accept as evidence of improvement."

Rayburn shifted in his chair, his eyes narrowing. "Why would that make so much of a difference?" he asked.

"Because we've not had any kind of goal before. Our former principals had their hands full just running the building, and there was never time to get really serious about student achievement or the conditions of learning. It's too big a job for just one person. Let us help you. Give teachers the power to roll up their sleeves and figure out the best ways to make things better."

Terri kept on going. "Our kids aren't bad; neither are our teachers. You tell us the goal and I promise you work like you've never seen before and you will see accomplishment. Think of it as the carrot-or-the-stick approach. If you do this, teachers will see it as a positive step, a sort of carrot. Your other approach would be treated like a stick."

Terri paused a moment before starting the final assault. "And, if you really want to look good, you'll make sure that you give us the resources we need to get the job done. It won't take a lot of money, but we'll need some. And the last thing—you'll need to stay out of our way. Leave us alone and we'll get the job done."

By this time, Terri's eyes were blazing with an intensity that made Rayburn think more carefully about his response. This was not going the way he had intended. But the idea appealed to him. If this woman could really pull off what she was saying, then it might be a win for everybody. He could put a feather in his cap and kids might actually learn something and give him less grief in the process.

"Okay," he said. "We'll try it your way. I'll tell you my expectation tomorrow morning. You'll have a week to tell me what resources you'll need—and 30 days to show significant progress. Now, if you'll excuse me."

Terri exited the office and rushed to her library. She needed time to compose herself before turning to the tremendous task that she had so boldly set forth. She had a thousand questions, all revolving around the reactions of her peers and students. Would they follow her lead or would they mire themselves in inactivity and endless argument?

Terri knew the answer as she took out a sheet of paper. She had confidence that good things could come of this. It may be a leap from being the school librarian to being the leader of school reform, but perhaps it made sense. After all, aren't library media centers the hub of learning, the information center of schools? Aren't professional librarians used to brokering services and building consensus? Is there any reason they can't assume the role of educational leader?

Lemonade does indeed come from lemons, she thought.

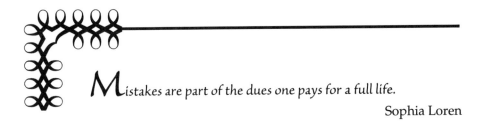

Mistakes are part of the dues one pays for a full life.

Sophia Loren

CHAPTER

14

Evaluation

We evaluate to learn.

This is the step that causes the most worthwhile reflection on all aspects of the plan and its accomplishment. This is the step that adds to levels of knowledge, leads to better planning for future goals, and creates deeper understandings.

Unfortunately, evaluation is also the step that is most overlooked (see Figure 14.1, page 132, for an evaluation checklist). The rush of life, with its concomitant pressures of time and influence, affects our judgment. We pay more attention to sound bites than to balanced analysis. We pay too much attention to our own prejudices and too little to accurate assessment. In short, we jump to conclusions in ways that perpetuate ignorance and demonstrate our foolishness. Consider this anecdote, which, by the way, actually happened.

Evaluation Checklist

Have I (circle one):

1.	Jumped to any hasty conclusions?	Yes	No
2.	Reviewed data along the way (formative evaluation)?	Yes	No
3.	Considered all informal sources of data?	Yes	No
4.	Considered all formal sources of data?	Yes	No
5.	Accomplished the major goal of the plan?	Yes	No
6.	Accomplished the minor goals of the plan?	Yes	No
7.	Considered any unintended consequences of the plan?	Yes	No
8.	Considered all the reasons for success or failure?	Yes	No
9.	Considered what could have been done better?	Yes	No
10.	Spent the time necessary to complete a thorough evaluation?	Yes	No
11.	Documented my evaluation in written form?	Yes	No
12.	Held myself accountable for plan success?	Yes	No

Figure 14.1   Evaluation checklist.

The Boy Who Ate the Worm

The school secretary came into my office. "Mr. Snyder, Mrs. Green is here and would like to see you."

"Do you know what she wants?"

"No, she just says that she has a question she would like to ask you."

I had spoken a few times to Mrs. Green at various school functions and knew that her son, Bobby, was a sixth-grader at our middle school. "Please show her in," I responded. "Let's see how we can help her."

After the usual introductory small talk, Mrs. Green got down to business. "Mr. Snyder," she said, "Bobby came home yesterday and told me that his teacher made him eat a worm . . . yes, a real, live worm." She must have noticed the incredulous look on my face. "Now I've been around children long enough," she continued, "to know that sometimes parents don't get the full story—and I would be very interested to hear the other side of this story."

"So would I," I responded. "Let's go talk to his teacher."

On our way to find Bobby's teacher, Mrs. Shepherd, I thanked my lucky stars that this mother was one of those rare parents willing to find out all the facts before making a judgment. She also looked as though she might even have the sense of humor that comes from raising a child or two.

A quick conversation with Mrs. Shepherd revealed this surprising scenario.

Bobby and his classmates were enjoying a morning field trip to the local park. Three teachers had joined forces to create a science workshop for their classes, which featured several different learning stations in an outdoor setting. The students formed groups and walked from station to station. Bobby and several of the boys in his group were changing stations when they noticed some night crawlers brought out by the previous night's rain. They promptly became more engrossed with the worms than with the science lesson.

Unbeknownst to the boys, one of the girls in the group alerted Mrs. Shepherd to the unauthorized activity. The frustrated teacher muttered under her breath, "If those boys like worms so much, maybe they'd like to have one for lunch." (Teachers are human, too.)

The little girl thought Mrs. Shepherd was serious and promptly reported what she had heard to the boys. "You guys had better get back to your station. Mrs. Shepherd says she'll make you eat those worms if she sees you with them again."

The boys ran, under the watchful eye of the teacher, back to join their group.

But they couldn't stand it. When the lesson got a little boring for them again, the same boys headed back to the worm pile. They must have been enjoying those worms because they didn't notice that Mrs. Shepherd was heading toward them. In fact, they didn't react until she was right on top of them. Bobby had a big worm in his hand. He looked up at Mrs. Shepherd with fear and trepidation. She glared at him and said, "Bobby, I want you to—"

Bobby didn't give her a chance to finish. He plopped the worm into his mouth, chewed it up, and swallowed it!

No one truly understands the workings of a sixth-grader's mind. Perhaps it was the prompting of the girl's earlier comment. Perhaps it was the fear inspired by his teacher's glare. Nevertheless, the deed was done. Of course, what the teacher was intending to say was, "Bobby, I want you to put that worm down and join your group."

How did Bobby's mother react? "I knew that there had to be some kind of explanation," she said. "Only my son would do something like that."

No, not really. Many of us have eaten the worm, figuratively, by jumping to the wrong conclusion. A thorough understanding of the principles of evaluation will minimize those embarrassing moments.

Formative Evaluation

Formative evaluation occurs along the way. It forms or channels thinking and actions as new data becomes available.

Intelligence-gathering and resource analysis are formative evaluators that can cause minor or major course corrections. A preliminary objective focusing on improving the attitude of a lead-bottomed administrator will change when it is discovered that the administrator in question will be retiring in six months.

Unforeseen barriers or opportunities can arise that create additional thought, which leads to additional data, the in-progress evaluation of which may reshape objectives and strategies.

Formative evaluation can be deliberate or incidental. Deliberate exploration and research may be necessary when strategies prove themselves ineffective. Incidental evaluation gives insight as realization either spontaneously occurs or slowly evolves.

Summative Evaluation

Summative evaluation happens at the end. It answers questions involving goal accomplishment and sets the stage for further learning. It provides valuable data on the "how-should-it-be-done-next-time" issues.

The most significant summative question is, "Was the goal accomplished?" An affirmative response usually indicates plan success. A negative response leads directly to seeking the reasons for failure.

Another significant question: "What were the unintended effects of planning and implementation?" These effects may outweigh all other considerations and are certainly the fodder for higher levels of learning.

The professional librarian seeking more support from a lead-bottomed administrator may find instead that the plan created even more animosity. Conversely, the plan could be more successful than anticipated when the administrator not only starts tuning in to library issues but becomes more involved in teaching and curriculum issues as well. The unintended side of life is the most interesting!

Informal Evaluation

Informal evaluation is most common. Our senses and thought processes sift data continuously, the results of which create the countless decisions that make up a day. The challenge inherent in this informality lies in how everyone perceives data. The garbage in/garbage out concept applies here. Faulty prejudices create faulty perceptions, which, in turn, create faulty judgments.

The most difficult challenge for everyone is acquiring information that can be trusted for its accuracy. That's why it is so important for professional librarians and other decision makers to cultivate a network of advisers who will give all sides of any issue, not just what the listener may want to hear. Although painful at the outset, bad news at the beginning of any focused problem-solving effort will eliminate more pain later. The analyzers of the world, although occasionally perceived as negative, are valuable resources. Their judgments may have a degree of accuracy that others won't have.

Formal Evaluation

Formal evaluation can diminish the chance of faulty judgment. It is the formal, after-action evaluation that is comprehensive, methodical, and documented. It compares data from pre- and post-assessments. It collects and analyzes objective and subjective data and appears in report form.

Written evaluation is key. Writing creates thought. The very act of taking the time to document an evaluation opens a person's mind to a host of issues that cursory, sound-bite judgment may gloss over.

Formal evaluation examines surface, intermediate, and application issues and focuses on personal accountability and learning.

Surface-Level Evaluation

Surface-level evaluation strikes at the heart of the plan and its accomplishment. It is summative in nature. It answers the question, "Was the mission accomplished?" If a plan contains a series of objectives, surface-level evaluation also renders judgment relative to the accomplishment of each.

Surface-level evaluation also looks for any unintended consequences that may have surfaced. (No pun intended.)

Intermediate-Level Evaluation

Deep thinking and good data are required at this level. Intermediate-level evaluation involves the exploration of the reasons why any of a plan's objectives were or were not accomplished. It examines unintended consequences in the same vein.

Sources of data should be varied. Students, parents, peers, and administrators may be consulted formally through data-gathering instruments or informally through conversation. Statistics may need to be developed and analyzed.

The most important source of information, however, is the planner; he or she must be willing to examine personal characteristics that may have contributed to the success or failure of the plan. All too often, human beings place blame on external events or people when it is really a character flaw in the planner/implementer that was most responsible.

Intermediate-level evaluation is generally the most time-consuming; if done properly, it is the most revealing. "You get what you pay for" applies to intermediate-level evaluation. A price paid in time yields better results.

Application-Level Evaluation

Application-level evaluation promotes learning by concentrating on how the lessons learned in the present can be applied in the future. It answers the question, "How could I have done this better?"

The application level focuses on personal accountability. It points a finger directly at the planner and challenges him or her to grow. This is where the rubber hits the road. Levels of commitment are assessed and decisions made that will determine future goal setting and accomplishment. In other words, application-level evaluations provide the framework for future plans.

Example

There was once a lead-bottomed administrator (LBA) who was goaded into activity by his school's student assessment scores. They were miserable. The LBA knew that a critical piece of any school improvement would depend upon the ability of his professional librarian to provide key services. The only problem was that the term *lead-bottomed* could accurately describe his librarian (LBL) too. Therefore, the LBA decided that he needed a plan to jump-start his LBL. (Are you still with me?)

Here's how the LBA went about it. First, he met with his LBL to ask for her help in providing more services to teachers and students. She readily agreed. Then he asked the LBL to solicit input from faculty and students and use that input in preparing a plan for increased services. The administrator gave the librarian a timeline, pledged resources, and expressed his confidence in her ability to make a real difference in their school.

The results were disappointing. The plan was shallow and insincere. Teachers viewed it as business as usual. The LBA decided on a formal evaluation of the entire scenario; he would model the evaluation along the lines of a great book he had just read. The plan called for both informal and formal evaluative processes and recommended documenting them in writing. It also called for surface, intermediate, and application levels of evaluation. Here's what the evaluation yielded.

Example 139

Informal Observations

Informal hallway conversations with teachers had warned the administrator that the prepared plan would not meet his expectations. He noted both the formative and the summative nature of the comments because they occurred during and after the plan's preparation.

Formal Observations

The LBA not only relied upon his own assessment of the completed plan, but sought the opinion of trusted advisers with expertise in library plans. He documented their comments and suggestions carefully.

Surface-Level Evaluation

The administrator's objective was to fully engage the LBL in the teaching and learning process. Although it could be argued that the LBL was already more engaged in the process, she was still not up to the level needed. Therefore, the administrator had not yet reached his unstated objective.

The first unintended consequence of the plan was that teachers were now even more convinced of the insincerity of the LBL. The second unintended consequence was that the LBA's own deficiencies in leadership were glaringly apparent.

Intermediate-Level Evaluation

The LBL's plan, upon examination, showed she had no vision for her library. Holding himself accountable, the LBA realized that he probably had not adequately prepared his librarian for success. The LBA was the leader in this situation and, thus, his was the greater responsibility. He didn't think it necessary to seek other reasons because it was painfully obvious that he was at fault.

This lack of leadership on the part of the LBA also related directly to the unintended consequences.

Application-Level Evaluation

The LBA should have better prepared his LBL for success. He knew that this should have involved first assessing the level of preparation of his LBL for such an assignment and then taking her to nearby library media centers known for excellence. That would have provided a forum for both of them to discuss the pros and cons of different ideas, thereby setting the stage for the LBL's conversations with their school's students and teachers.

The LBA knew, too, that he needed to deal somehow with the negative attitudes of his staff toward his LBL. After thinking it over and speaking again with some trusted advisers, he opted to focus his energies on improving the work ethic and skills of the LBL. Results spoke louder than words with his teachers.

Summary

Evaluation creates thought, which leads to learning. Effective evaluations are written. They rely on good data sources. They include formative and summative components. They can be informal and formal. Formal evaluation examines surface, intermediate, and application issues and focuses on personal accountability and learning. Comprehensive evaluation can save the embarrassment of jumping to the wrong conclusions.

Case Studies

Readers probably thought they were finished with Alan Reed and Terri Sanchez; but read on to hear about their analyses and learning.

Alan Reed

Alan's principal looked tired, his voice attempting kindness. He started off by saying, "I've heard that you're running quite a process down here. Something about advice to the lovelorn. Care to fill me in?"

Caught by the moment, Alan first asked his principal to sit down and then blurted out the whole story. He finished by asking his principal for advice and noted the irony of the question. Although he had intended to evaluate his own plan, his principal was going to do it for him.

"After a lot of years in this business," his principal began, "I've come to one conclusion. Although there is tremendous satisfaction in working with kids and teachers, none is greater than enjoying your own family. Although your methods may be somewhat unorthodox, they reflect some serious thought. Keep working in the direction you're going. You won't be sorry."

Alan's relief was evident. He started to say something but was interrupted by his principal's getting up to leave.

"And one more thing," his principal said. "Let me know if you need some help."

Terri Sanchez

Terri was too excited to spend time on evaluation now. Besides, time would tell more about her success or failure than introspection at this point. She realized, however, that she had indeed survived the meeting and turned Dr. Rayburn's thoughts in a different direction. This was success.

The real work lay ahead.

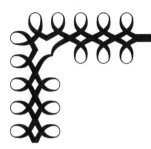

Part III

Strategic Ideas

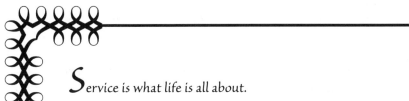

Service is what life is all about.

Marion Wright Edelman

15

Building Relationships

One of the grand keys to personal and professional success is building better relationships with all stakeholders of your library media center—administrators, teachers, parents, and students (see Figure 15.1, page 146). Remember, the idea is to help your boss look good and she or he, in turn, will do the same for you. It's the old art of politics—you scratch my back and I'll scratch yours.

Building Better Relationships

One extra thing that I could
do this year for:

Administrators

Teachers

Parents/Community

Students

Figure 15.1   Building better relationships.

There's an anecdote that illustrates this principle.

Old Crenshaw had lived a good life. Honest, hardworking, and faithful to his wife and family, he finally died at the ripe old age of 93. He must have arrived at the pearly gates during break time because there was no one to greet him. However, he noticed a door labeled "Hades" and, upon closer inspection, saw a note on the door that said anyone could peek in. A naturally curious individual, Crenshaw did just that.

What he saw was awful. A large group was seated around a banquet table filled with every kind of delicious food imaginable. It was truly a feast fit for a king. The only trouble was that the feasters looked as though they were starving to death. Crenshaw saw why. They all held forks with handles so long that they extended past their mouths. The forks could not be used for eating. The people made every attempt to feed themselves, but could not.

Crenshaw closed the door, hoping fervently that he would not have to go there. Then he noticed another door marked "Heaven" and saw the same invitation to look inside. He was astounded to see the same setup—table, feast, people, and long forks. The difference was that the people were all smiling and obviously enjoying their feast. Then he saw why. They were all using their forks to feed the people sitting across the table from them. The forks were just the right length for that.

The moral of the story is obvious. We survive and thrive in our families and professions by serving others. Then, the "what goes around comes around" principle kicks in and our service to others is most often returned to us many times over.

Here are some ideas. They are simple and doable, and professional librarians will only be limited by their imaginations in birthing the 1001 exciting and creative ideas not mentioned here.

Ideas for Building Better Relationships with Administrators

Lunch. Arrange for a quiet spot. Bring a special sack lunch or take your boss to a restaurant. Involve kids or teachers if that will help. Give your boss a written invitation and state your agenda. Express your appreciation and solicit support. Build relationships and trust. Don't do just one lunch—or breakfast—do them every now and then.

VIP Treatment. Find out what books, journals, or movies your boss likes and give him or her first crack at them. Let your boss know that you serve others in the same vein; then make sure you do. Everyone wants to be a VIP. Great people make everyone else feel as though they are.

Awards. Administrators always like awards and it is human nature for an award recipient to live up to the reason for the award. Write recommendations for state or regional awards. Make up small, but meaningful, local awards. A blue ribbon with a card attached for "outstanding service to the Columbus High School Library Media Center" will brighten anyone's day. If appropriate, notify the press.

Personal Letters. A thank-you note goes a long way. So does a hand-written letter. How about a nice letter to the boss of your boss?

Letters to the Editor. Public recognition works. Everyone likes to feel valued. Letters to the editor also highlight the importance of libraries.

Read to Kids. Invite administrators to read to elementary children. Have a special chair for that purpose. Invite the press if appropriate.

Judging. Invite administrators to judge any kind of competition in the library media center. Or set up different displays and ask administrators to judge the merchandizing effectiveness of them.

Skits. Write and perform a skit for a school "no-talent" show—even spoofing your administrator (or your professional relationship with the administrator) if appropriate.

Presentations. Invite your boss to present with you at a conference of some sort. This shows respect for his or her talent and facilitates skill building.

Ask Advice. Ask for advice or counsel on any matter deemed appropriate. Don't overdo it, but people are generally flattered to know that their opinions are respected and sought.

Volunteer. Principals are always hunting for people to fill committee slots. Let your principal know that he or she can count on you.

Secretaries. Cultivate good professional relationships with the principal's secretary. You never know when you can use an ally.

Key communicators. Publish a monthly newsletter or user-friendly report that can be sent to the principal and other key communicators to highlight all the good things that are occurring in the library media center.

Meeting Facilities. Offer the library media center and any equipment needed for meetings. Help administrators run the equipment.

Speakers Bureau. Run an informal speakers bureau. Encourage administrators to recognize the library media center as the source of important information and facilitating.

Results. There is no substitute for great results—especially in students' achievements. It is much more credible to market substantive work.

Ideas for Building Better Relationships with Teachers

Relationships with teachers can make or break a professional librarian. In many cases, reputations will rise and fall based on teachers' perceptions and cooperation.

A word about teachers. Most entered the profession out of an intense desire to work with children. Union negotiation stances to the contrary, they did not become teachers to make money. They wanted—and want—to be known as builders of children. They are among the most altruistic people found on earth.

As such, they are extremely sensitive to the needs of their students. However, this heightened sensitivity also extends to themselves. They will immediately note any instance of perceived unfairness and take it personally. Librarians must be aware of this and deal with it.

Another thing to keep in mind is the different personality characteristics detailed earlier in this book. Teachers can be explorers, pioneers, and settlers; introverts and extroverts; left-brained and right-brained; concrete-sequential and abstract-random; promoters, perceivers, analyzers, controllers; Type A, Type B, and any combination thereof. (This author hopes that all preservice library programs offer a good course in the psychology of teachers!)

Here are some ideas that may help library media teachers develop and maintain great relationships with their classroom teachers.

Personal touches. People always appreciate small acts of kindness. Finding just the right instructional aid, acceding to a last-minute request for equipment, and a personal note or card of encouragement at difficult times all let the receivers know that you respect them and care for them.

Resist rigidity. Although rules and procedures are necessary for most library media center operations, they can discourage rather than encourage. Don't hide behind the rules. Sell yourself and the services that the center has to offer. Make allowances for people who never seem to be able to make a request on time, and appreciate even more those who do.

Awards. Teachers love stickers, and attaboy and attagirl notes, and "teacher of the week" pins, and "friend of library" certificates, and door prizes, and free bookmarks, and, and, and, and . . . This is a great way to keep morale up and spirits motivated toward supporting libraries. Assign a trusted student aide to be the "chief of creativity" in coming up with a steady stream of ideas.

Socials. Teachers like to talk and have fun. Sponsor get-togethers frequently. Highlight new books, periodicals, or equipment. Show off different aspects and services of the library media center. Get teachers in the habit of knowing that a half-hour of fun and refreshment will always be interrupted by a *short* (five-minute) commercial about the library.

Helen (Nitsa) Demos, highlighted previously in this book, passed on these next two ideas for after-school socials:

> *Upon arrival at school one morning, each teacher, staff member, and administrator found a ripe banana in his or her mailbox with a tag that read, "Bring this banana to the media center after dismissal today." When they got to the library, the new books were on display that had been received from a $5,000 grant written by the media specialist. The banana was used to go with all the ice cream and trimmings provided for banana splits. The principal funded this afternoon treat after we had convinced him that food was a great enticement for teachers to preview books.*

> *Several years ago, our school plan for the upcoming year was to include Whole Language. The principal funded professional materials for the media center when convinced that the library needed to support the school's plan. To ensure that the faculty previewed the new materials, the teachers received a tube of Lifesaver® holes in their mailboxes with a note that read, "After school today, come see the "hole" thing in the media center." The Whole Language materials were on display along with donut holes and soft drinks, again funded by the principal.*

Curriculum. Establish the library media center as the curriculum center of the school. Keep extra copies on hand and become the expert on their contents. This will also help professional librarians know what resources can be developed to assist teachers. Librarians should be as familiar with curriculum content as subject-area teachers.

Professional development. Reserve a portion of the library media center for professional development materials for teachers. Then stock it with the really good stuff that teachers want to use. The idea is to get them to hang out where the information is. Libraries should be the information and communication hubs of schools.

Mailboxes. Have a mailbox for teachers and put surprises in it. A piece of candy, a note, or some trinket or other will always bring teachers back. They crave positive attention—especially in these hypercritical times!

Contests. Put together contests—complete with prizes—that highlight collection size (guess the number of books in the library), most books in the library by a single author (who's the author?), the genre represented by the most books, the weight of the biggest book, authorship of an obscure quote, oldest book in the library, and any number of other ideas. The student "chief of creativity" can help here, too.

Door prizes. "Congratulations, you are the fifth teacher to enter this library today!"

Even a lowly bookmark given as a prize can lift the spirits of teachers.

Lunch. Teachers like lunch, too! Prepare a special box lunch or go to a restaurant. Have a special point or two to make but concentrate more on building relationships and trust.

Ideas for Building Better Relationships with Parents

Too few librarians tap into the power of parents. A parent turned on to reading sets an example hard for children to resist. This example or "picture" can have more effect than the thousands of words preached by librarians and teachers in encouraging students to read. Here are some ways for professional librarians to engage this often-forgotten group:

Friends of Libraries. Given the right mix of leadership and participants, a library advocacy group can accomplish the improbable. Such a group can raise funds, reach out to other parents, engage students, and apply political pressure. A brainstorming role can complement their barnstorming role because they can be a veritable wellspring of ideas and innovations. They will require nurturing and hard work by professional librarians, but the results are worth it.

Key communicators. Everyone wants to feel special. Develop a key communicator mailing list for parents unwilling or unable to participate in a Friends of Library organization. Send copies of newsletters or news items to them. Use them for surveys. Meet with them once or twice a year to solicit their opinions. A key communicator concept list can be the training ground for a Friends group.

Another aspect of this is the general communication from the principal's office to parents. Try to have some small piece about library media center activities in each mailing. A library calendar of events can be particularly useful.

Parent volunteers. Good parent volunteers are priceless. They can help with clerical tasks, read books to children, assist with student research projects, make displays, and even be the friendly greeter at the door. Mark Twain commented on the gentlemen stagecoach drivers in eighteenth-century England who drove the most arduous routes for sport, not for pay. Parent volunteers fall in the same category. Nurture them and enjoy them and they will perform tremendous service for libraries.

Business partnerships. Join civic groups and cultivate relationships with local businesses. Perhaps they would consider adopting your library media center or some portion thereof. Give them credit and generous publicity when due.

Special events. Book fairs, poetry readings, mystery clubs, and support groups for science fiction, Civil War, and fantasy aficionados can all create enthusiasm. Invite the mayor to read to parents with their children. Sponsor skits or plays. Keep an eye on commercial booksellers to see what promotional ideas they generate.

Contests. As with contests for teachers, figure out ways to engage parents through the same medium. Children could earn tickets to go toward a drawing for a book gift certificate. The class that brings the most parents to the library over a month's time could win a prize. Children are the best leverage. Get them excited and they will sell the concept of libraries to their parents.

Personal invitations. There is no substitute for a personal touch. Professional librarians can earn great amounts of credibility by sending personal notes to parents. Note topics are endless, but good news is best, for example: "Thanks for raising such a great daughter. She is really interested in learning and has been a good example for her peers." Purchase a generous supply of custom-printed note cards to facilitate spur-of-the-moment note writing. Make sure that you display your library's logo and mission statement in a prominent place.

Lunch. To create strong bonds with a parent, share a few private moments over a meal.

Awards. Parents like awards, too!

Ideas for Building Better Relationships with Students

Students are the easiest to engage. They have a natural enthusiasm for life untempered by seriousness. An added benefit is that an excited student will bring five friends. Wise professional librarians covertly draw from this energy to recharge their own batteries. The greatest challenge lies in providing direction to these perpetual-motion machines.

That's one side of the story. The other side concerns the growing number of students suffering from serious attacks of lethargy. (I saw this little gem of graffiti scratched into a desk once: "Before I got here, I didn't know what apathy was. Now I don't care.") Waking up even one of these students and inspiring an enthusiasm for books brings a reward greater than a paycheck.

Special events. Kids like anything that breaks normal routines, and most librarians do a terrific job at creating all the little contests and events that excite children. Here are some ideas that are just a tad out of the norm.

How about an Abe Lincoln Day where children have to walk five miles just to get a book? Try a mountain climb for older youth punctuated with extracts from the latest Himalayan expedition. Or a high school media class making a library commercial for elementary students. Or an activity to create a culinary masterpiece taken from a published recipe. Or a book-signing party for students who have been published. Speaking of students being published, library personnel can be special promoters and encouragers of students' efforts to write and be published.

How about librarians collecting students' verse and formatting and publishing it? That could make quite a project for a Friends of Library group; it could also be profitable.

Mozelle Waters used to ask students where in the world they would like to travel if they had unlimited time and money.

Then she would find literature about that country or area and encourage her students to find out more about it.

Another technique that she used was to find groups of friends and encourage them to select a topic of interest. Then she would find them each a book on that topic and have them trade the books around until they had read them all, thus creating literature discussion groups.

Contests. Kids are people too! They like contests and the chance to win something. Contests can be so much fun that it is a shame to restrict the results to library media centers; instead, join forces with other teachers to stimulate their programs, too. The art teacher may want to help kids sketch a banana split for your "best banana split" design contest. Of course, the winner and runners-up should receive gift certificates for ice cream. History teachers may want to sponsor "History Hunts": teams of youth descend upon the library to answer a list of 20 questions. (Don't forget to invite the principal to be the referee.)

One time-honored contest is to encourage students to learn at least one new word every day; the one who comes up with the most interesting word wins the daily (or weekly) prize.

Door prizes. Another natural for youth! Prizes could be specially marked bookmarks that entitle the finder to a special prize. Or a few dollar bills spread out in some rarely-read tomes with a note attached that says, "Anyone reading this deeply deserves a dollar!"

Key communicators. High school and middle school youth have a lot of ideas—and some of them are good ones! A newsletter just for them (written by a special student assistant) can gain great dividends.

Respect. I once met a student in the hallway of an alternative school who had dropped out of a traditional high school a couple of years before. I asked what brought him back. His reply? "My mom was nagging on me to come back to school so I came here. I wasn't going to stay, but everybody gave me respect right from the start. That makes a big difference. This is the only school I've been in that gave me respect." He graduated shortly after that. Library media centers whose personnel respect all students will pull in some of the most surprising ones.

Recruiting a handful of at-risk students as student aides ties in with this concept. A partnership between librarians and at-risk youth can create strong bonds. These youth are starved for the right kind of attention and will be loyal to a fault to any librarian who exhibits a true interest in them. A caution here—librarians may have to change some of their long-held attitudes toward kids who come from different backgrounds and display different behaviors. Again, respect is the key.

Environment. Retailers work hard on their floor displays and attitudes toward customer service. Their profits depend on doing a good job in both areas. Library media centers sporting welcome signs and posters are friendlier. Sincere smiles are absolutely necessary.

Hours of operation. A customer-friendly environment may necessitate figuring out a way to keep the library open longer. Students can build stronger relationships when they have time to engage in that communication unfettered by school schedules and ringing bells.

Suggestion boxes. Although many suggestions will be frivolous, sometimes a real gem shows up. Everybody likes to have an opportunity to give input and this is one way that is fairly easy to support. It also gives library personnel another way to recognize good ideas and their sources because a small prize rewards the best suggestion of the month. Thank-you notes can be another way to recognize suggesters who at least gave it a try.

Service clubs. Middle and high school service clubs are generally on the lookout for good service projects. Encourage them to adopt a portion of your library media center. They can solicit ideas from their classmates, raise funds, and purchase attractive items. Obviously, this partnership will reinforce the service clubs' personal connections to the library media center as well.

Lunch. Did I mention that kids like lunches too? It makes them feel special.

Web Sites

Web site technology has brought with it a host of public relations opportunities suitable for reaching all stakeholders, that is, administrators, teachers, students, parents, and community members. Be sure to look up the national and state sites applicable to school libraries. (The American Library Association has a particularly good one.) They not only give valuable ideas on how to sell the importance of library media centers but they tip you off on what things to include in your own Web site as well.

Summary

Service is the key to building relationships with administrators, teachers, parents, and students. Ideas for service come from keen observance of local circumstances and imaginative response.

Respect is a common theme for everyone. Professional librarians who exude politeness and respect in their every word and deed will build solid relationships and trust.

Time is a crucial issue. Professional librarians should exercise the wisdom of Solomon in choosing or creating activities that will foster good relationships without unduly sacrificing other priorities.

God don't sponsor no flops.

Ethel Waters, jazz and blues singer

Gaining Credibility

Rome wasn't built in a day. Neither is the credibility of professional librarians. A good stew requires (1) high-quality ingredients, (2) a variety of ingredients, and (3) a lot of simmering. Professional educators need the same. There is no substitute for quality, variety, and experience.

Here are some do's and don'ts that may help the beginning professional librarian get off to the kind of start in a new position that supports personal growth toward that quality, variety, and experience.

Do

Listen more than you talk. It may have been Mark Twain who said, "It is better to remain silent and have others think you a fool, than to open your mouth and remove all doubt." Some people talk incessantly. Others expend more conversation in criticism than in praise. Be wary of both styles. The best compliment is "She listens and hears what I say."

Remember who your boss is. Educators are fond of telling students, "It is your job to get along with your teachers, not vice versa. That's the way it is in the world of work, too." We should probably heed our own advice. It doesn't hurt for us to remember that we are not the easiest personalities to get along with, either.

Come to work a bit early and leave a bit late. The educator who beats the students out the door at the end of the day is universally denounced. A few extra minutes each day shows a willingness to go a little extra on behalf of the employer. It also makes up for the time that may have been inadvertently wasted in idle conversation during the day. True professionals give a full day's work for a full day's pay. Now, now, no rationalizing here. It is incumbent upon every employee to give a full measure of work regardless of how much we may think ourselves abused by the system. If nothing else, we should remember the many contributions made by employers toward our retirement and health, disability, and workers' compensation insurances. Sick and personal leave are benefits. So are long-term disability policies and sick-leave banks. And what other employer offers a cafeteria lunch for less than three dollars?

Of course, the greatest privilege is that of spending the majority of our time working with future generations—and getting paid for it. What a deal!

Look for opportunities to serve. Initiative is valued by all employers. Just as with individuals, organizations are never stagnant. They are either progressing or regressing. Employee initiative creates a momentum for success that ensures both individual and organizational progression.

Study your profession. Professional growth comes only through study and experience. Those active in professional organizations renew understandings and develop new ones. Visits to other schools and library media centers unlock doors to networking and more knowledge. Many great librarians are shameless thieves of good ideas—and they share their own ideas with others.

Develop your own unique leadership style. The myriad characteristics unique to a particular individual make up formulas for success. We can't force ourselves to fit another's mold. Successful educators recognize and rely on their strengths while compensating for their weaknesses.

Don't

Talk more than you listen. This one bears repeating. Learning does not take place during speech. Credibility decreases in direct proportion to increases in verbal output. If you're not sure whether you talk more than you listen, try this test. Sit down to lunch with several students or peers. Then keep track of how much time each one spends talking. If you take more than your share of time, or if you feel the urge to take more than your share of time, you probably tend to talk more than you should.

Criticize. The only people interested in the half-baked judgments of inexperience are those with agendas counterproductive to unity and collaboration. Holier-than-thou, know-it-all attitudes quickly destroy credibility. If you think yourself a tad critical, try this test. Monitor your own speech during a day and count the number of times you render a negative statement. If it's more than three, you have a character flaw that needs improving.

Abandon integrity. The first year on the job establishes personal values. Yielding to the enticements of dishonest peers can destroy credibility. Professional librarians hold positions of trust in schools and communities; they must stay squeaky clean in all their dealings. Pay attention to proper accounting procedures and controls so that you avoid even the appearance of dishonesty.

Integrity of thought and comment is just as important. Students and teachers share their thoughts if they believe that confidences will be respected. Conversely, they will stay away from people who spread the rumors and vagaries of school life.

Show favoritism toward teachers and students. Showing favoritism swiftly erodes trust and credibility. Both teachers and students are very insightful when it comes to how they are being treated, and they will immediately pick up on someone else's favored status. Those who perceive themselves in the "out" group will unnecessarily avoid the library media teacher—an action fraught with lifetime consequences in terms of literacy and learning.

Developing a Marketing Plan

There is no substitute for substance. There is, however, value in marketing. Sometimes people (bosses) just need to be educated about what really represents high-quality performance in a library media center position. One way to do that is to create a personal marketing plan.

George Doolittle was the nondescript librarian of George Washington Elementary School in a small community somewhere along the Atlantic seaboard. He was just shy of 50 years old and long overdue for a midlife crisis. He thought he was a pretty good employee but noticed that the fire and enthusiasm of his job seemed to be missing.

Then it happened. He received a notice that he was now eligible for an AARP (American Association of Retired Persons) card and that it was in the mail. That pushed George over the brink.

He went home in a blue funk and laid it on the line to his beautiful and wise spouse. "Wanda," he said, "I can't stand it anymore. Every day I go to work, take care of kids and books, and then come home. My principal doesn't notice me and neither do the teachers. The kids do, but it's only because I'm the guy who takes care of the books. My life is at a standstill."

Wanda calmly responded, "George, the way I see it, you've got two choices. First, you could quit your job, withdraw our life's savings, buy a boat, and sail around the world."

Wanda noted the glint in George's eye and decided to move on quickly. "Or, you could examine your job and figure out a way to make it more exciting. After all, you're still quite young, dear, and I have a feeling that you've not even come close to reaching your true potential."

George definitely liked the first option better but decided that he had better give the second one a shot. Fortunately, he had just bought a great book that had a lot of good advice about planning for success. He picked it up and started reading. It wasn't long before he was engrossed; he soon started to think about how to apply some of the things it was saying to him.

The sections on assessment, setting goals, and creating a marketing plan particularly interested him.

Assessment

The first thing George needed to do was a needs assessment (see Figure 16.1, page 164). That way, he wouldn't have to rely on his own judgments about his personal strengths and weaknesses and those of his library media center. Not one to get bogged down in paperwork, he put something together that seemed fairly user friendly and gave one to a colleague as a test case. His colleague completed it and returned it with some suggestions. George made the changes and then sent it out to all the teachers in his building.

The assessment instrument first asked easy questions relating to the availability of library media center services, personal friendliness, library instruction, environment, communication, and so on. Then it dug a little deeper by soliciting suggestions for improving services.

George expected people to be generally satisfied with the services that he offered, but was surprised to discover that they felt his library program needed more excitement and energy. Indeed, the comments of his peers reflected his own evaluation. He was stagnating in his position. He also discovered that many of the teachers were not aware of all the services his library media center offered.

Informal Customer Satisfaction Survey

I am a   Teacher   Parent   Student
(circle one):

Rate the following on a scale of 1 to 5—5 being the highest or best level.

In the _____ library media center:

- I receive friendly service.   1 2 3 4 5
- There are enough books and materials.   1 2 3 4 5
- The learning environment is pleasing.   1 2 3 4 5
- The displays are informative.   1 2 3 4 5
- There are lots of extra activities available. 1 2 3 4 5
- I receive frequent information.   1 2 3 4 5
- I am a satisfied customer.   1 2 3 4 5

The best things I like about the _____
library media center are:

One suggestion that I have to make about the _____
_____ library media center even better is:

Name of person filling out this form (optional):

Figure 16.1   Informal customer satisfaction survey.

He decided to follow up on the needs assessment by personally visiting with the teachers in his building. He even checked in with a few parents because he hadn't taken the time to poll them.

One-on-one conversation reinforced George's thoughts about revitalizing his program. Teachers felt that it was a good program but that it could be better. It was also obvious that they weren't aware of the variety and depth of available services. Parents were especially interested to learn about services for them.

The last poll that George conducted was with his principal. Mary Doherty was a young, energetic instructional leader whose only weak area was library media centers. Just in her second year of a principalship, she hadn't yet taken the time to figure out what she wanted from George and the library program. His conversation with her created some real thought and contemplation about how George could play a pivotal role in improving instruction. Her energy was infectious and George even felt some of his old fire coming back as Mary started brainstorming possible strategies with him.

Goal Setting

George knew what he needed to do. Although his present program would probably need some fine tuning along the way, it was really pretty solid. His main need right now was to inform teachers and parents of what he had to offer and involve them in using his services. As that happened, the "fine-tuning" suggestions would naturally come forth and he could carry them out as he saw fit.

Marketing Plan

Getting the word out to teachers and parents meant that he needed to prepare a marketing plan. This plan would, he hoped, inform, educate, and engage his teachers and parents in using the services of the library media center. The only problem was that he knew little about marketing plans. So what did George do? He consulted a marketing expert.

Lyn was experienced in school public relations and had such a good reputation that she was able to start her own consulting business. Although it cost George and his budget a few dollars, he felt it was a good investment to have Lyn's help in creating a high-quality marketing plan. She came to his library media center, talked with George, and visited his principal. Then she gave George some sample plans and a list of ideas tailored to his situation. It looked as though George was getting a good handle on the concepts, so Lyn wisely withdrew and told him to call her if he needed any other help. She left with a final note of encouragement and also asked for a copy of his final product.

George took Lyn's ideas and samples, sat down at his word processor, and started to create his plan. It was exciting! The ideas were flowing and he once again felt the fire returning. Here's the plan he developed.

George's Marketing Plan

Goal: Inform, educate, and engage teachers and parents in using the library media center services at George Washington Elementary School.

Strategies:

1. Maintain a substantive, full-service program worthy of marketing.

2. Inform staff of goal by preparing and personally distributing professionally printed note cards listing library media center services and giving home phone number.

3. Inform parents of goal by preparing and mailing a one-page flyer describing library media center services available to them.

4. Create awareness among teachers of personal consulting role that I can fulfill for them. Have business cards printed up that say, "George Doolittle—*Your Personal Instructional Consultant,*" and promote that service whenever appropriate.

5. Work with the principal in sponsoring monthly get-togethers for large and small groups of staff. Topics may include workshops of interest (staff development in techniques for teaching core subjects plus elective areas), reviews of the latest book and video arrivals, just-for-fun social gatherings, and literature dialogue groups.

6. Work with the principal in sponsoring monthly get-togethers for large and small groups of parents. Topics may include workshops relating to parenting (adolescent development, discipline, etc.), reviews of the latest book and video arrivals, just-for-fun social gatherings, and literature dialogue groups.

7. Work with the principal and teachers in sponsoring special activities for children and for children with their parents (readathons, dialogue groups, storytelling, etc.).

8. Prominently display a suggestion box.

9. Prepare a monthly newsletter for teachers, parents, and students regarding library media center happenings and plans.

10. Find a high school student to create a George Washington Elementary School Library Media Center Web site and keep upcoming events posted on it.

11. Create a George Washington Elementary School Library Media Center logo and use it everywhere. Create a marketing slogan, too. (George Washington LMC— *Where the Action Is* came immediately to George's mind.)

12. Review library media center entryway and interior for "welcoming" signs and make sure that fresh ones are displayed.

13. Purchase pens, pencils, and other tokens that can be used for prizes and gifts. The library media center logo and slogan should be printed on them.

14. Keep principal informed every step of the way.

Evaluation:

1. A formal needs assessment will be done annually for teachers, parents, and students.

2. Informal customer satisfaction surveys will be done quarterly for teachers, parents, and students.

3. The principal will be consulted frequently for advice and evaluative comments.

George was excited. He believed he had taken charge of his life and his career and that he would once again look forward to going to work each day.

Wanda was excited, too. She had not been looking forward to sailing the world in the tiny boat that could be purchased on a librarian's savings!

Summary

Professional librarians gain credibility by listening more than talking, respecting their employers, demonstrating a solid work ethic, looking for opportunities to serve, studying their professions, and developing unique leadership styles.

Professional librarians lose credibility when they talk more than they listen, when they unduly engage in criticism, and when they abandon integrity.

George Doolittle discovered that rejuvenating his library media center and his career depended on a commitment to needs assessment, goal setting, and creating a marketing plan. He reinforced his understanding that library media centers never stay the same—they are either progressing or regressing. He also learned that progression is incremental and relies on constant change. Effective marketing plans encourage a two-way flow of information that creates healthy and nonthreatening conversations leading to improvement.

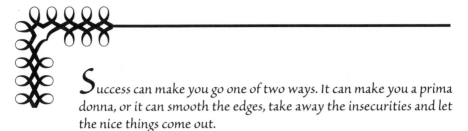

Success can make you go one of two ways. It can make you a prima donna, or it can smooth the edges, take away the insecurities and let the nice things come out.

Barbara Walters

CHAPTER

17

Personal Satisfaction

Library media specialists have every right to savor their successes. They are hard won in an environment that is competitive and critical. In the rush of life it is easy to forget what those successes are.

Successes

Some are spectacular in terms of their visibility. Successful fund-raising for acquisitions or construction falls in this category. So does the organization or rejuvenation of a Friends of Library support group. Engineering a major shift in administrator, staff, student, or parent attitudes toward library media centers is a great accomplishment.

Some successes may not be quite so visible but are nonetheless important. Turning a youth toward a love of books and lifelong learning brings tremendous satisfaction. There can be no greater reward for an educator than to have now-grown men and women return and say, "You were the one who made a difference for me. Thanks." In terms of the eternities, that experience is greater than any paycheck. Money comes and goes. Influence for good is passed from generation to generation.

Although some may seem minuscule, when the cumulative effects of many small actions are taken into account, they contribute to progress. A kind word here and a small act there can make a student's day go just a bit better—or a teacher's, or even an administrator's.

Of course, the contribution made by professional librarians toward individual learning is their bread-and-butter success. Knowledge empowers youth. It enables, even fuels, their drive toward responsible adulthood and successful lives. It gives them the confidence to confront difficult issues and resolve them. And, of course, it affects future generations as today's youth give the gift of knowledge to their own children. What a privilege to be part of something as noble as that!

Challenges

The end of any school year is particularly hard on personal and staff morale. How many times have tired educators said as the year was winding down, "The morale in our school has never been so bad." Then the usual finger-pointing occurs. Generally, the principal or central office administration receives the blame. Although they are accountable for their share, probably nine months of pressure-laden work has more to do with fatigue.

Professional librarians, just like all other educators, are being asked to do more with fewer resources of time, personnel, and money. Again, there is the old saying that describes the human service environment that educators find themselves in at this time: "We have done so much for so long with so little that now they expect us to do the impossible with nothing!"

The competing interests of lower taxes and greater expectations will continue to squeeze public servants. Professional librarians must find their own balance in this equation. Their careers can be challenging and fun, but at the point where the fun disappears it is probably time to think of a change. Everybody has a different level of tolerance for life in the trenches; there is no shame in that. In fact, it can be a real opportunity for continued personal growth and satisfaction as old skills are used as the base for building new ones.

Balance

Self-motivation and enthusiasm can tip the scales toward accepting the mounting pressure. Many people thrive on adversity and in effect say, "There's no mountain I can't climb. Bring it on!" These are the explorers and pioneers among us.

Others seek to settle down, to find that balance that allows career fulfillment plus family and personal fulfillment. These are the settlers. It takes all kinds to make an exciting and challenging world. Explorers, pioneers, and settlers all fulfill vital roles.

Note, too, that people change. The traditional model is one of exploration and pioneering at the beginning and middle stages of careers. Then age and wisdom combine to create a different perspective and settling down occurs. However, some people never change: they seek new challenges until the day they die. Some people start off with balance and then decide to strike off in new directions.

It takes verve, innovation, tenacity, and an abundance of wisdom to be a settler. Achieving just the right balance is often dependent upon a mix of people, circumstances, and events that are not easily controlled.

The story of Alan Reed and his approach to seeking that balance is instructive. He held himself accountable for influencing his situation and discovered that it is possible, albeit fraught with its own challenges.

Caution

It is easy to rationalize a lack of commitment and even just plain laziness by unjustly pointing toward family and balance. Clock-punchers, daydreamers, and time-wasters need to commit themselves to more work so that their lives aren't overbalanced with their personal interests.

So do sick-bay commandos. These employees take every single day of sick and personal leave afforded by their employing schools and are masters at looking for every policy loophole to have more time off. Although a relatively minor percentage of employees fall in this category, they harm the reputations of the rest.

There are self-serving reasons for all educators to make sure they are giving as much as they possibly can to their professions. In these hypercritical times, a real danger exists that public education as we know it today will disappear. If public schools are dismantled, those that staff them will go, too. Educators everywhere must prove their worth to taxpaying publics. Professional librarians, administrators, and other school employees who shirk their responsibilities and fail to give the full measure of their talents will do nothing more than contribute to the demise of not only a great service to American youth but the organization that provides employment and sustenance for our families.

That being said, let's get on to addressing the needs of the vast majority of professional librarians—those who are working too many hours, feeling too much pressure, and needing a little more balance in their lives.

Achieving Balance

Verve. This descriptor connotes energy and enthusiasm in tackling difficult issues. It is a force seldom denied by lead-bottomed administrators. The inertia of bureaucracy is no match for a dynamic, supercharged professional librarian on a mission.

Cindy was one such librarian. Over the 15 years of her professional life, she had amassed a number of accomplishments. Her high school program was solid and everyone knew it. She had created effective processes and programs, and many of her peers noted her singular devotion to the cause of literacy.

Ted was her principal. Rising slowly through the ranks, he had served as assistant principal for 10 years before assuming his present post three years ago. Cindy had always gotten along with Ted, primarily because her accomplishments made him look good.

Cindy's oldest child was entering middle school (a traumatic event for any parent) and that caused her to think about the amount of time she was spending at work versus the amount of time spent with her children. She decided that she needed to make some minor adjustments in her work habits to better accommodate the needs of her family.

She had two choices. She could go ahead and make the adjustments and, in all likelihood, Ted would never notice. Or, she could be up front with Ted and tell him what she was planning and why. She opted for the second choice. It was a better match for her leadership style and she knew that Ted was no match for her extraordinary verve.

Innovation. Cindy knew, however, that verve is better when mixed with healthy doses of innovation and substance. So she came up with a plan that would actually strengthen her program while allowing her a more flexible schedule.

A high performer all her life, she was not particularly adept at delegation. And, like many controllers, she found that it was often easier to do something herself rather than rely on others. Delegating some of her responsibilities to a trained cadre of library workers and volunteers became the centerpiece of her plan.

She put it together and presented it to Ted. He didn't stand a chance. Not completely ignorant of the realities of school politics, he recognized the plan for what it was—an opportunity for an employee to gain skills, fulfill family obligations, and allow others to grow professionally and personally. There were no downsides. It was win-win for him.

Tenacity. But Cindy recognized that the enthusiasm and excitement of the moment can disappear as old habits and the pressures of the job create hard choices. She had to stick with her plan and that would be hard.

Fortunately, Cindy had been an educator long enough to see many examples of children whose parents were too busy to support them. She knew that her children needed her even if they said they didn't.

She also knew that the old rationalization of quality time being better than quantity time was false. Special moments of quality occur spontaneously, most often at unpredictable times. Quantity time gives more opportunity for quality moments. The two hours spent by a parent watching a child participate in a game or other activity may be rewarded by only a quick hug. No matter. That 30-second moment of recognition would not have happened without the two-hour investment of time.

Cindy had focused on her priorities to maintain the balance that she knew she needed. She also fine-tuned her plan every now and then to make sure that she was doing the best job she could in both her professional and personal lives.

Wisdom. The only thing constant is change. It is inevitable. Organizations and the people who comprise them change. Students and parents change. As individuals age, they change. The irrational judgments of youth give way to enlarged perspectives. Parents are always harder on their older children than on their younger ones.

Wisdom reflects a person's ability to create and/or adapt to change. It also enables people to experience the joy and satisfaction that can accompany each stage of a person's life. People with lives in balance are perceived to be wise; they have the ability to take a step back and contemplate their roles in the larger perspectives of professional and personal lives.

It could be argued that a lack of balance in one's life reflects a lack of wisdom.

Summary

Library media teachers achieve many successes, some more visible than others. Student learning is the primary goal. Everything that contributes to that represents success. The best evidence of that success comes when former students return to say "thanks."

Public education is stressful. Its challenges are daunting and can cause professionals to rethink their commitments. Career changes can be healthy. Balance between professional and personal lives is necessary. Some educators may use balance as an excuse to further shirk responsibilities, but they are in the minority.

Successful balance takes verve, innovation, tenacity, and wisdom.

Professional and Personal Worth— Final Thoughts

Professional librarians, library media specialists, and library media teachers rank among today's heroes. They carry the torch for literacy and knowledge. They open doors to life. They pass the keys of success to anyone willing to possess them. No other individuals occupy such positions of privilege.

Every epitaph of every librarian should read, "Here lies a contributor to society."

Index

from **LIBRARIES UNLIMITED**

LESSONS FROM LIBRARY POWER
Enriching Teaching and Learning
Douglas L. Zweizig and Dianne McAfee Hopkins

Use the profound changes instituted by the Library Power Project as a catalyst for the revitalization of your own school library media center. An invaluable instructional model.
xiii, 281p. 8½x11 paper ISBN 1-56308-833-9

THE EMERGING SCHOOL LIBRARY MEDIA CENTER
Historical Issues and Perspectives
Edited by Kathy Howard Latrobe

This compilation gives you an in-depth understanding of the school library movement through personal and objective perspectives. The authors address the mission of the school library program and how its realization has been shaped by a variety of factors.
xiv, 288p. 7x10 cloth ISBN 1-56308-389-2

100 LIBRARY LIVESAVERS
A Survival Guide for School Library Media Specialists
Pamela S. Bacon

Save time and make your job more manageable. You'll find advice on overwhelming issues including how to handle overdue materials, establishing a book club, teaching Internet research skills, and improving public relations.
xxi, 317p. 8½x11 paper ISBN 1-56308-750-2

MANAGING INFOTECH IN SCHOOL LIBRARY MEDIA CENTERS
L. Anne Clyde

Learn how to develop and effectively manage the *right* information technology plan for your SLMC. Clyde addresses the full spectrum of available technologies and emphasizes applications in the areas of management, services, and curriculum.
xiv, 290p. 7x10 paper ISBN 1-56308-724-3

For a free catalog or to place an order, please contact Libraries Unlimited/Teacher Ideas Press.
Phone: 1-800-237-6124 • Fax: 303-220-8843
E-mail: lu-books@lu.com • Web site: www.lu.com
Mail to: Dept. B025, P.O. Box 6633, Englewood, CO 80155-6633